Purpose for the Pain

A COLLECTION OF JOURNALS BY RENEE YOHE

Published by Bonded Books, Inc.
1030 North Orange Avenue, Suite 105, Orlando FL 32801
David McKenna
Jack Thomas

BONDED BOOKS

Written by Renee Yohe
Cover design by Maven Creative
Book layout by Studio AKT
Edited by Adam Smith

www.PurposeForThePain.com
www.BondedBooks.com

First Edition
First Printing August 2008
Printed in the United States of America

ISBN 978-0-615-22318-6

For it is shameful even to mention what the disobedient do in secret. But everything exposed by the light becomes visible. This is why it is said:
"Wake up, O sleeper
Rise from the dead
And Christ will shine on you."
— Ephesians 5:12-14

It is our way to look at that which is shameful and hide it so that nobody can hurt us or think less of us. It is rare to take those shameful things, those shameful thoughts, those shameful deeds, those shameful abuses, and lay them in all their nakedness, sadness, darkness and painfulness for all to see. Yet, that that is what Christ did. He laid himself before the world until death. And then, He rose. So we, like God, are called to lay ourselves open for Him to raise us from our deaths, the death of our heart, memories, souls, actions, reactions, bodies and minds.

And so, Renee, follower of Jesus, in her way lays her deaths before us here in pad and pen so we can see her darkness. And there in her darkness we can hear God whisper,
"Wake up, O sleeper
Rise from the dead
And Christ will shine on you."

-Kelly Winkler
 Renee's Counselor

ACKNOWLEDGEMENTS

To my family who built me up with laughter and words of wisdom, who cushioned my fall with welcoming arms and tender kisses, who spent many sleepless nights and tearful days loving me and dealing with my absence; my heart could never find the words to tell you how sorry I am for the pain I caused, and how grateful I am that you fought for me. You are the foundation, the launch pad, the safety net, and the cheering section for my life. I love you a thousand times over.

Ryan, my faithful friend. Thank you for believing in me, for being something I could hold on to when my world was shaking.Thank you for being a compassionate heart, an ear to hear across the line when I said everything was fine, and we both knew what that meant...thank you for standing by with a lifesaver when I know all you wanted to do was jump in.

David. If there were ever a time to invent new words it would be now, so that I could somehow tell you what a godsend you are in my life. Thank you for being "the good bitch" when I needed one. Thank you for speaking into my life. Thank you for restoring my faith in humanity. Thank you for being a warrior on my behalf, a man of action and wisdom. Thank you for being the vessel that God used to give me a second chance at life. Through your transparency God spoke to me that night and started me on the first steps toward recovery. Then He brought you back into my life with a community and a love more powerful than I had ever known, and you had the strength to hurt with me as I banged my head again and again in addiction. You let me flail until I wanted help, and when that moment came, you were there to fight the world for my life. I will forever be grateful for you, what you have done for me, who you are to me now, my dear, dear friend, and the role you have in my future. Thank you.

To Erin, my other half. I owe you a lifetime of Taco Bell and countless cartons of cigarettes. You will always have a piece of my heart and my life. Your friendship has taught me more about myself and what it truly is to love than anyone I have ever known. You have taught me what it is to be patient, to hurt, to fight, to try, to earn that depth we so desperately long for, to believe in another human being. You have a heart of gold and I am so blessed to have a part of it. Thank you for picking me up out of hell and loving me enough to bring me back and let me go. Thank you for waiting for that day that I didn't want to live there anymore. You have loved me more fiercely and truly than I could have ever hoped, and that has made all the difference.

Kelly, I could never thank you enough for the years you have invested in my heart. You have pushed me, hugged me, and sat with me through some of the hardest things I've ever faced. You have gracefully allowed me to rip apart your blankets, stain your shirt and fidget my way through many hours with you, and never gave up hope that I would one day choose to take a hand and look into the mirror and fight. Thank you for understanding my heart like no other.

To every person who opened their doors to me, to every mother who cared for me as their own, for every prayer, every ride, every meal, every pair of shoes...to the lady and her beautiful family in that Denny's who bought me breakfast several years ago, to the treatment centers and halfway houses and the incredible people who work there, and to all of the friends who walked through this battle with me, THANK YOU.

To my beautiful boy, you have walked my heart through a million graveyards and shown me that it is safe to love. You have patiently sat there and let me claw at you after many intense counseling sessions and held me when I couldn't stand. You softly defy every haunting memory I have associated with men and no "thank you" could possibly equal what that means to me. You truly are a gift.

Above all people, places or things my heart longs to acknowledge my Savior, without whom things like hope, love, redemption or purpose cease to exist. It is my daily blessing to wake up and know that He is responsible for this new life that I have, and the beautiful people in it. For all the days that started dark and rainy there have been rainbows. For all the tears that have been shed, something has grown. For all the wounds that have been made, there is a beautiful scar to be shown, and for the hundreds of nights my soul has wandered He has welcomed me home a thousand more.

"For I know the plans I have for you," Declares the Lord,
"plans to prosper you, not to harm you, plans to give you HOPE and a FUTURE."
— Jeremiah 29:11

...Thank you.

FOREWORD

My story is one of alcoholism, addiction, depression, and ultimately, redemption. The afflictions I endured would send me down a path of overdoses, treatment centers, incarceration, and subsequently, through grace, make me the person I am today. I had a wonderful childhood with a family anyone would be blessed to have; yet I still went down a road of darkness. I am fortunate to have parents who stuck with me through all the darkness that I may eventually see the light. Had they let me go, that light may never have been realized. It is through love, friendship, Alcoholics Anonymous, and an undying faith that I am alive, healthy, and successful today. There is much more to my story; it could be an entire book of its own. Perhaps another time. Another forum.

I first met Renee Yohe in 2005 when speaking at a young-adult church service in Orlando, FL. A few weeks before, I had met the pastor of my church, AJ Sherril, over coffee. While I had been attending Status for some time, this was the first time I had the opportunity to meet and speak with AJ. He immediately wanted to know my story and I offered it to him in the Reader's Digest version. His eyes continued to widen as I spoke, and it was clear he was shocked by what he was hearing. He asked me if I would be willing to share my story in front of hundreds of people. As I had done it elsewhere a few times before, I had no hesitation in agreeing. As we wrapped up our time together, AJ's next appointment walked in. I was introduced to Josh Loveless, who just returned to Orlando after working for Willow Creek Community Church in Illinois. I knew of the Loveless family as Josh's father David was/is the pastor of Discovery Church, Status' parent church. Josh had started the student ministries years earlier, and was returning to oversee them once again.

Josh called a few days later and asked if I would be available to share my story at an upcoming service. He explained his concept to me. The service would begin with a video of me telling of the dark days—about ten minutes of pure darkness. I would then walk out on stage right as the video came to the most intense moment of my story. Josh would interview me about what happened in my life that brought me to sobriety, and where I'm at in my life now. It was quite dramatic. It would also be the first service Josh would be a part of since returning to Orlando.

The video was shot in a local recording studio where I did quite a bit of work and had done my first internship years earlier. A large mixing desk was the background in this professionally shot video. As requested, I arrived early for the service and was introduced to the staff, as well a tall, smiley, and sweet guy named Jamie Tworkowski. Jamie was scheduled to do the announcements that night as well as introduce the service, the topic of which was redemption. All involved in the service had a brief meeting outlining the evening followed by prayer. Then Josh Loveless and I met one-on-one to discuss everything in detail. We prayed again and my one prayer was the same as always: If even one person in the room was affected, then it was worth opening up and revealing things that are scary to make public.

The service went exactly as planned. Jamie made a great introduction. The video was intense, and the interview was the perfect follow-up that exemplified the story of grace and redemption. At one point during the interview, Josh told of a friend of his who came to him recently. This friend told Josh of his friend, who was talking about suicide and furthermore, actively "cutting herself." Josh asked me what I would do or say to someone in a situation like that. What advice would I give to the friend?

Immediately following the service, a guy I had met a few times before approached me. I had met Ryan Kirkland before as I had been a judge in a few battles of the band that the church had held. In the most recent, I had voted his band, Between The Trees, the first-place band. Ryan told me that he was the friend Josh had spoken of, and it was his friend who was cutting and suicidal. Coincidentally, that friend was in service and wanted to speak with me. I told Ryan that I would love to, and he informed me that she was waiting in the green room, high and coming down off of a cocktail of drugs. I immediately found peace in the idea that one person was affected that night, and that I, in some small way, might be able to have an impact on someone's life.

Ryan, Josh, and I headed back towards the green room. Waiting there was a fragile, petite, beautiful, broken girl. She was shaking like a leaf on a tree. I felt sick to my stomach about what she must be experiencing, as I had been down the withdrawal road many times before. I introduced myself, and began to ask questions. She rambled on and on in a drug-induced babble. None of it made much sense, but strangely I understood everything she was saying. She told stories of many things I have experienced, and some I haven't, including rape. This was an area to which I had no response. What do you say to someone who shares that with you?

After listening for quite some time, I began to talk. I talked for a long time, which I tend to do. I don't remember all that I said, but I do remember two things in particular. I told her "you're done," and repeated it several times as I stared into her eyes and I began to tear up. I also told her that one day, her story was going to change and save lives. I was definitely right about one of those things, and unfortunately, wrong about the other. I don't claim to be a prophet, exemplified by my 50 percent accuracy that night. By stating that her story would change lives, I simply meant that by sharing her story one day, it could have an impact on people just like mine did that night. Who knew what her story would eventually become and how many lives it would truly affect?

The following day, Renee would leave for a treatment center in South Florida. The following week, Renee's parents would come and seek me out, thanking me and stating that they had their first real conversation with their daughter in years after she returned home from spending time with me. Renee would live in the treatment center for the next two months. Following that, she would spend three months in a halfway house.

During her tenure in South Florida, Renee and I would keep in touch and our friendship began to develop. With every conversation we had, she sounded better and healthier. I also maintained a regular dialogue with her parents. While worried, they were thrilled that their daughter was getting the help she needed.

When Renee left the halfway house to return to Orlando, she was healthy, vibrant, and excited about life, or so it seemed. She began to attend a regular small group at my house, and built a support group that consisted of some amazing friends. Seemingly, she was in counseling, excited about life, and on fire in her faith. Everyone was optimistic, including me. I know how easy it is to fall back into things, even immediately after a treatment stay. What I didn't know is that she already had.

Renee's visits to my small group would eventually become infrequent, as did her church attendance, and her phone calls. There was a period of a few weeks where I couldn't get in touch with her at all. During this time, I was speaking with her parents who hadn't heard from her either. Needless to say, we were all concerned. We couldn't find her, and when you can't find an addict it means they're either on a binge … or dead. I believe there are two potential fates for drug addicts: sobriety or death. We were scared that it was the latter.

One night at about five in the morning, my cell phone rang. Without even thinking, I answered, "Hello, Renee. Are you okay?" She was quiet and then began a rant that went on for about ten minutes, and I just listened. Finally, I interrupted her and asked if I could come see her. She refused but agreed to meet me for dinner the following night.

The next night, I picked her up from a "friend's" house. She got in my car and stunk of booze, and her eyes looked like they were falling out of her head. Nothing I wasn't familiar with as I personally looked like that many times before. Through all this, Renee still looked beautiful and harmless and innocent.

We had dinner, and Renee shared with me what she had been doing, and why she had been doing it. There were fresh razor wounds on her arm, and she told me she had no interest in stopping any of it. Why would she? She's young and having fun, as she told me. I told her that I would be there for her no matter what, in any condition she may be in, as well as under any circumstances. I never wanted her to not call if she was in trouble, or simply to talk.

The weeks continued and the late night phone calls were commonplace. I would listen to the rambling until I couldn't listen anymore, and then offer to come pick her up wherever she was. She would refuse, and that is usually where the phone call ended. We would do the periodic meal or coffee with the same conversations every time. She was simply not ready to walk away from the lifestyle.

She would periodically show up to church or small group, every time completely trashed. Never was the level of her intoxication subtle, rather always overt and obvious. Once in a while she would try to hide it, but for the most part she just didn't care who knew or what anyone thought.

My breaking point came late one Sunday night after a church service. Several of us were sitting in a Bennigan's restaurant waiting on our food. One of our friends received a phone call, talked briefly, and stated he was leaving to go pick up Renee. He left and returned thirty minutes later with Renee, stinking like booze and stumbling all over the place. I asked her to come outside with me and we sat on a bench and smoked cigarettes.

I opened my heart up to Renee. I told her that I couldn't do this anymore; that despite what I had told her, that I would always be there, that I would never abandon her, I simply couldn't take it anymore. I was running a business and the all-night phone calls, the constant worry, and all the stress was beginning to take a toll on my life. I began to feel like this situation was compromising my sobriety and recovery. To spend time with someone and think that cocaine, my drug of choice, could be sitting in her pocket at any time, an arm's length away, was just fucking scary. Never did I think I could abandon anyone like that, but I had to be sure I was okay. If I relapsed, what good could I be too anyone?

I gave Renee two options. She would either need to return to treatment or I would have to remove myself from her life. I explained the reasoning behind the latter and she understood. She was in a pickle. She didn't want me out of her life but she sure as hell wasn't stepping foot back in a treatment center. She had many questions and concerns. The main one being that there is no way she could afford it. I immediately put that concern to rest by telling her that I would pay for it. At the time, my business was doing well and I was in a position to do so. It took quite a bit of conversation before she finally said that she'd go. It was an emotional moment and we both shed quite a few tears. However, there was no way she was going to leave that night.

We were still a few days out from what would be the beginning of her treatment stay. We were also a few rough nights away.

By this time, the pastor I had shared a coffee with, AJ Sherril, and the nice tall guy, Jamie Tworkowski, were both living with me. Several months earlier we would all meet the same week, Jamie and I the same night. Renee and I, coincidentally, the same night as well. Also, the Pastor whom I shared a stage with, Josh Loveless, was now one of my best friends. The singer of Between The Trees, Ryan Kirkland, was now my dear friend, and client, as I was now managing his band.

One night, my new roomies, our friend Ashley, and I were hanging out in my living room. We were all on the couch watching TV, and Jamie sat at the dining room table on his Macbook, as he often did. My phone rang and it was Renee. She sounded a complete mess; more so than usual. I talked to her for a while, and we were making plans for her treatment stay, which would begin the next day. I told her I was worried that she wouldn't make it until the next day, but she assured me she would be fine.

The phone conversation ended and AJ, who also knew Renee quite well, asked if we should go see her. I didn't think it would do much good but thought it to be a good suggestion. Ashley, who had recently met Renee, wanted to see her as well. We called Renee back and she agreed to see us. As we were getting ready to go, Jamie, who had never met Renee, asked to come along. Those who know Jamie know that he has a heart of gold, seeks any opportunity to help, and genuinely hurts when he sees the pain of others. He would be a great addition to the group.

We got over there, talked, prayed and I threatened the lives of the people she was staying with. The rest of the story has been well documented in Jamie's story.

Josh Loveless suggested that I allow others to contribute to giving money for Renee's treatment, and I agreed. We started with our small group and our church. There were several people who made quite generous contributions. As Jamie's story began to draw a following, he suggested selling t-shirts to help contribute. The rest is history.

Almost three years later, no one could have had any idea that these events could lead to something so great. I can only speak of my life and my observations, so that is what I will offer here.

AJ has moved on to plant a church in Long Beach, CA, called "Origins L.A." He is doing well, and from everything I hear, so is the church.

I funded and marketed the Between The Trees album securing me a distribution deal with Fontana Distribution, Universal Music Group's independent distribution arm. We then upstreamed the record to Universal Motown, making us the first Universal independent label to upstream an artist to a Universal major. The Between The Trees boys are some of the most important people in my life and I have dedicated much of the last three years to developing them. Two of the songs on their album, *The Story and the Song*, are about Renee. "The Way She Feels" and "A Time for Yohe" were written long before anyone knew who Renee was, including me. These were songs inspired by Ryan's friendship with Renee and his personal experience with her, and "The Way She Feels" was the first BTT song ever written. I am so proud of these guys and what they've become (more importantly, who they've become).

Josh Loveless is my pastor and close friend. He works with me at my different ventures and he even A&R'd the Between The Trees record.

"To Write Love on Her Arms" has grown beyond anyone's belief. The organization is changing lives and helping people the world over. I firmly believe this is currently the most powerful word in the world educating our demographic on substance abuse, self-mutilation, and depression. Jamie and his team are spreading the word and letting people know they are not alone. I feel that the organization has become what it has because, simply stated, the world needed it.

Renee has become a woman. She is beautiful, healthy, and working with others to change their lives based on her experience. It is amazing and emotional to look at Renee now and think of where she came from. Perhaps it is a small glimpse of what my parents see when they look at me now. God, I put them through hell. I couldn't be more proud of Renee.

Last year, I went through a stumbling block in my life. It was a very scary one, and one that I never want to walk through again. Again, another time, another forum. I will say that after going through this extremely challenging patch, Renee was there for me as I was for her when she needed it. I remember meeting her for a movie, and sitting in the bed of her truck afterwards. She spoke words of encouragement into my life that I will never forget. She is an integral part of my health and happiness today, along with God, my family, and a few close friends. Full circle I guess.

Renee, like all of us, has dreams. Her immediate dreams are to write and to speak in a way and in a forum that would allow her to change and save lives. Over the last few years, Renee has come to me and ask me to help her with her goals and desires related to her career. Simply, I didn't think she was ready. Several months ago, Renee and I were having a coffee. She told me that she was ready, and quoted me on having told her several times that she is one of the healthiest people I know. Who was I to hold her back? She was ready.

I began to tell her everything she would need to start writing this book; a plan, an outline, an editor… Then she interrupted me. "David, the first book is already written." Needless to say, I was both intrigued and impressed. She then told me of the journals that she's been writing in for years, how the entire Renee Yohe story has been documented for the last five or so years as she was experiencing life. There were physical journals, emails, livejournals, MySpace blogs… the list goes on.

I couldn't help but think of the amount of lives that her story has already affected; how her story of darkness, and eventual light, in its entirety, could change more lives.

We formed a publishing company, brought on a project manager, hired a real editor, and began a journey of several months of hard work. Of course, many of the pages have been omitted. This was necessary in order to protect the innocent, as well as the guilty. Mind you, in no way is this watered down, and in no way is this for the faint of heart.

Someone once told me that coincidences are God's way of remaining anonymous. There are too many of these things to simply ignore in this story. Dreams have been realized and lives are being changed. Over the last year, I have been seeking like never before in my life. I've been asking questions, and not simply believing everything that is told to me. I want to know firsthand. There are times when I question my faith and my purpose. I must never forget all the "coincidences" that continue to happen in my life as well as those around me.

-David B. McKenna
Orlando, Florida

INTRODUCTION

I would be tempted to give you a "Once upon a time..." introduction to my life story, but that would be too pretty and typical. While I did have your average pastor's kid meets missionary kid childhood, there was something different, something dark, even in the beginning, and I guess that is typical too. We all come into this world kicking and screaming, regardless of how loving or caring an environment we are brought into. I kicked and screamed my way through early childhood and into my teenage years despite my wholesome family life and the safety of the walls I lived inside of. There are other walls to speak of. Walls I built to keep people and pain out, and to keep me in, all in one piece and untouched by the stab of change. Walls I began to build to protect myself from the world in all of its ugliness, and the ugly people in it. I began to taste its ugliness at a very young age. I also began to taste other things, other forms of escape as I began to run. The bittersweet drop of sweat on my lips was far more pleasant than the tears I could have been crying.

My life can be broken down into a few basic themes; foundation, running, destruction, and most importantly, redemption. My childhood years, the family, church and friends that poured into my life, formed the foundation—the home—for me to return to in my later years. I was brought up in the church, where I could fit God in a pretty, gift-wrapped box and love Him with abandon. Then my parents' hearts were called to the mission field in Moscow , Russia . Thus began the building of my first wall (a wall to keep the pain out), and the first of a series of late night fist fights with my pretty God.

I threw myself wholeheartedly into sports and social events, anything to stay busy, keep moving, keep running. Anything to protect myself from feeling the pain of my upcoming move. I taught myself to compartmentalize everything that hurt. If I never had to sit still in silence, all the noises I'd been hiding from couldn't catch up to me. My mind was in a constant state of chaos, struggling with depression and untreated bipolar as well as the normal frustrations of a young teen. I was a social butterfly, an exceptional athlete and student, and regular youth group attendee. My outer shell was aesthetically pleasing, while my insides were a steadily growing cemetery. At first glance, you would ask in bewilderment, as many often did, "What was so bad?! You had everything you needed, just what was SO bad?" I wondered this too for years, unable to explain the train wreck sitting inside of me. It just didn't make sense. It didn't fit. There were other internal catalysts that made this masterpiece.

When I think of twelve, I think of miniature people and carefree days and goofy clothes. My twelve was all of those things, but it was also isolation and an introduction to self harm. It was an unsuspecting dance into shame and dirt and sweeping and rugs. There, in that first moment where I chose to crucify my pain onto my forearms, I discovered a new way of running. I had been fighting with my family and was sent to my room; my childhood was filled with temper tantrums and time outs, and in the time I was confined to my bedroom something switched. The action came to me like a vision, or a movie, I could see myself taking the glass from my windowsill and using it to cut my arm, and just like that, I stumbled into a losing battle for the next eight or nine years. My parents caught me that day, and the look in their eyes made me feel as if they were the ones I had actually cut. I think we were all in shock, none of us knew how to deal with it, so we never really did. The problem seemed to vanish with the scabs. The burden of being found out kept my vice dormant for several years in which I entertained uppers and downers and eventually found what would become the loves of my life: alcohol and drugs. I didn't return to cutting until after we moved to Moscow. My first drunk, I was a freshmen in high school. It was all in good fun in a situation I assumed to be "safe." I was shamefully proven wrong. The night ended in vomit and lost clothes and lost friends and statutory rape. Another good reason to run. Harder. I was too afraid to drink anymore but the move was getting closer and closer and the pain became more real, I needed to escape so I began to get high. I used to escape, and it seemed every time I used something else would happen, giving me another reason to run, so I had to use more, thus each high perpetuating this downward spiral toward complete destruction. My family soon moved to Russia , which is a very dark period of time in my memory, as is most of my high school years. Self-harm became a nightly routine for me and my depression was at its peak. Cutting failed to purge my pain and my drinking increased, especially since liquor was easily obtained in a country where it was so socially acceptable. I struggled with disordered eating and entertained thoughts of suicide, all under a guise of self contentment and a healthy sense of humor. I hid my pain from my family for nearly two years because I didn't believe my feelings were of any importance compared to their missionary work, and I feared the repercussions. When I finally confided in my parents after a close call, we picked up and moved back to Orlando where I began counseling and continued on my path of self-destruction.

We moved back after New Years of my junior year and I quickly got my act together for the sake of my family and old friends. However, the memories of the friendships I had kept so close to my heart, where not what I had fantasized. Things had changed and moved on without me, where I had frozen time where I left. The pain of returning to a home that wasn't home soon sent me back into my old vices. I had worked hard in school and participated in youth events, but I was still struggling with cutting. Eventually it was back to my old ways, my pain had been growing like a weed inside of me and I embraced it. In doing so I chose to throw away many opportunities and healthy answers. I dug away at my pain with a vengeance. I. lost. Everything. I was on a one-way street headed the wrong way with no clue how to turn around. Every Cinderella dream, every white dress and promise ring, every comfy house with its safe walls and clean beds, every laugh and song, was gone, down the drain half-dead in a ditch somewhere waiting to be found, hoping to be salvaged. In the span of my senior year in high school I managed to lose my home, and most of my friends because of my self-destructive nature. The school considered me emancipated so I took full advantage and left whenever I chose. I began to care less and less about classes and sports. When I wasn't at school I was crashing parties and walking the streets. I spent my nights couch surfing. Several people attempted to take me in, but it never lasted very long. I slept at whatever party I'd ended up at, whoever's place that had picked me up off the street, whatever park bench or slide seemed safe, and ended up passed out in ditches or staying on doorsteps when my friends weren't home. I learned what it meant to be taken, to give carelessly, and lost all respect for people, myself and my body. If I wasn't abusing it, someone else was, and the saddest thing was that I believed I deserved it. Hope wasn't something so strong and beautiful as we make it seem sometimes. In retrospect it was some distant shore I would think about, or try to clamor toward. It was the few faithful friends who stood by me and let me word vomit all over them because they couldn't do anything else.

Before there is new life to be had, there is death; a series of events, like the changing of seasons, the breaking of walls and the hitting of heads on counter tops. My change began locked up in a glass case with ace bandages and people who talked to themselves as they paced the halls. At eighteen I was Baker Acted twice within a month and placed in a psychiatric ward. It also began with a counselor and Arby's and a picture of me and my skeleton clothes-hanger body holding a yellow sweatshirt in our first attempt to seek treatment. It began with a boy with a voice and a guitar and telephone calls just to say "I care" and "I'm there" and some songs to carry me through. Some late night talks on docks and walking through his neighborhood and just being whatever we were. It began with faithful parents with open arms and the suggestion of a rehab center in Fort Lauderdale shortly after I was released from the psych ward for the second time. It took my love for them when my love for me wasn't strong enough to say yes, and go. It began with a man with a past like mine and his story and his prayers ringing in my ears the night before I was to leave for the first treatment center, and his promise to be there and surround me when I came out. I fought my way through that first rehab center and opted for a halfway house where I lived for three months. I made friends I'll never forget, I learned lessons that changed my heart and mind, built a few solid steps into true recovery, and I had my first taste of stability and health in a long time.

But, I wasn't there to quit. And I didn't. I thought I would be the exception to the rules and I could use, just once, just for fun. I quickly found out that I was just like everyone else and I went back. I went back this time with a busted face and a neck brace lying on the floor without a purse. I was mugged when I had nothing to give and they beat the last of the fight I had in me right out onto the concrete. The police never caught the men who beat me, and I suffered from post-traumatic stress. I couldn't continue living there, so I moved back to Orlando , my stomping grounds. I ran harder than I ever had before, because now I had the truth. Once you know the truth it lodges itself into your throat every time you take a drink, swallow a pill. It lays down on top of your arm when you pick up a knife and it's never the same. There is a hole in your self will ... that power you once had to control, to build, to run, to escape, has weakened. So I sprinted headfirst into it as hard as I could. But then, there were bumpers in place, a girl who told me we would be best friends, who came with food and hugs and nothing but love when I was nothing but drunk. A girl who would buy my cigarettes just to buy some time. A girl who would pick me up every Friday night and take me to a house filled with people who lifted my name and listened to my drunken reasoning with promise and hope for something more to be there one day. That man, that man, that godsend of a man, stood alongside me in all of my peril and, when I was drowning reached down and punched me in the face. Knocked me out! He reached out and carried me to shore when I was willing to be there. My new beginning came when I finally wanted an ending. I finally began to see the vicious cycle I was stuck in. I didn't have answers, all I knew was that I was tired and I wanted out. I had to want it, that was the key. When I did, there was this beautiful gift called community that came along with open arms and open hearts and held my hand while I walked the line into new life. David came to me with the suggestion of treatment after one night that entailed me locking myself in a closet with a bottle ready to give up on life. He sent a friend to come and rescue me from my jail cell. We sat outside a restaurant and discussed some sort of plan to give me another chance. A fresh start, the help that I truly needed. It seemed impossible, far away, ridiculous, but at that point I had no better ideas to offer. David offered to pay for my treatment if I committed to sixty days. I approached this proposition with the heart that if God wanted me there, all He had to do was open the door and I would walk through it. Doors did open—not when or how we thought they would—but they did and I began my journey into a new life.

The treatment center would not take me in the first time we arrived, and quite frankly I wasn't fighting to get in either. I had my doubts. It took several cigarettes and some hard ultimatums to get through the application process. I made it through with my nose bleeding and my hands shaking and David right my by side. I was declared too great of a risk and wasn't expected to make it through the five day waiting period, but I rode it out in the company of some loving friends and returned to the center a second time. From day one it was a battle to wake up, to participate, to care about people or myself. Rehabilitation is no vacation. There were days I wanted to leave, days that I conjured up escape routes and pit stops as I walked to the bus stop for work. I watched many girls leave that house, and to this day don't know what came of them. I fought through many sleepless nights and scratched my way through nightmares as the memories I buried in booze and drugs slowly awoke from their graves. I rejoiced in others' recovery and shared what I had when I could. I learned and loved and began a healing process that will continue for the rest of my life. I spent three months there before moving to Fort Lauderdale to live under the wisdom of an old counselor of mine. Even in recovery I lost much and experienced some of the most painful events of my life. Just because we get sober, it doesn't mean that life gives us a break. With my counselor's guidance and the support of an ever growing community that formed out of my five day detox, I grieved the loss of an old roommate I had had at the halfway house. I soon moved back to Orlando and began life as recovering addict. I found work and learned responsibility. I learned simple life skills I had lacked like cooking and cleaning, and even got my first car. Just one day at a time—sometimes one moment at a time—I made my way through each day living this new way. I have been walking this line for just over two years now, two of the most beautiful, awful, wonderful, terrifying years of my life. I have fought harder than I've ever fought for anything, I have cried harder, laughed, and screamed louder, and grown in the most painful, fantastic ways. Today I choose to feel the pain of sitting through a feeling, the terror in realizing that I am powerless over so many things, and the joy in knowing that I do not experience these things alone. I fight my feet when they beg me to run and battle my mind in its attempts to protect me from remembering the things I worked so hard to forget. Today I choose to fight, to stand in front of the mirror and let God hold my hand as I wake up the dead and face them head on. Today is a constant war for healing, and today is filled with promise and potential. I have dreams and goals of changing the world, of leaving a true legacy of love and redemption. I long to be a catalyst for a revolution.

But, the most beautiful thing about all of this is that this redemption I've experienced was not my own doing, but that of One who is far greater than I. It is not my hands that keep my arms from scars or my mouth from quenching its thirst in pretty poison. It is a God who loves me, who carries me when I am too weak, and He has been, He always was. I just wouldn't let Him. The hope that I had in Him was the rope that I clung to through the darkest of days. When I was in high school I met a girl who introduced me to this prayer, "God, make me a shining star in the universe, give me ears to hear, eyes to see, and a heart to understand."

This has been the prayer of my heart, my hope. The idea that God could take the ugliest, darkest corners of our lives and expose it, make our secrets transparent and shine through them, is what fuels me. I want nothing more than to share my heart with the hope that God would take my pain and give it purpose, beauty and use it to redeem those that may find themselves somewhere in these pages. There is a purpose for the pain. It is called redemption.

-Rene Yohe, July 30, 2008

`03

★

— SCRATCH AND DENT SALE —
I HANDED YOU THE KEY TO LET YOU IN,
YOU NEVER TOLD ME YOU WOULDNT
LEAVE ANYTHING STANDING
(YOU LEFT NOTHING STANDING)
YOU TRASHED EVERYTHING AND
TOOK ALL THAT I HAD
THE SAD THING IS I WOULD HAVE
GIVEN IT TO YOU IF YOU ASKED
(WHY DIDNT YOU ASK)
SO NOW I SIT HERE AMIDST THE RUBBLE
AND I THINK THAT I BLEND IN
MY HEART BROKEN- IN PIECES
SCATTERED MEANINGLESSLY ACROSS THE FLOOR
A PATHETIC TRAIL THAT LEADS ONLY TO U
(AND I WONT FOLLOW)

And I'm damaged goods
Mark the price down
Redline sale — fifty percent off
(Cuz no one buys)
Who will want me now?
But go ahead to your trophy room
And add one more to your collection
Another check on your pricy
Shopping list — and now on
to the next item....
(Is that all I am?)

— Priceless Flaw(s) —

Perfection is surrealism, a lofty goal, set so high that no one can see it and we're left to speculate and conjure up in our imaginations just what exactly is it? A distorted ideal, a biased opinion, and where do we draw the line, and when do we cross it, and why? All i know is that ~~everything that reflects, in~~ in falling we learn to fly ~~⬤⬤⬤~~ ~~⬤⬤⬤⬤⬤⬤⬤⬤⬤⬤⬤⬤⬤~~. So i'll let your lies stab out my eyes until my heart can see, watch you come closer (so i can push you away.)

TO ███ — ПОШОЛ НАХОЙ

ask me why my stomach hurts,
why i stare out from bloodshot eyes
ask me to explain the burning
in my throat and that bitter
sweet aroma that follows me.
ask me why i cringe under ur gaze
why the longsleeves in this heat,
if this is perfection,
ill cling to my flaws and
gratefully announce defeat.

PITIFUL GRAVE   Aug 30 '03

How did I come to be here,

back in this hole

i thought i crawled out of,

again at the bottom,

covered in dirt,

sweat and tears,

every movement is agony,

i think my heart is bleeding to death

you're slowly draining my feelings

and injecting bitter resentment,

apathy and callousedness,

are the major side effects,

the cure-all is the dark,

that sweetly falls on retired souls,

and gently parts them from their pain.

The wretched pain of unfulfillable longing,
holds me writhing in its steel grasp,
stabbing contemptuously into me,
my heart is bleeding to death,
and all they can do is slap on a band-aid,
this is my tragic love story,
concieved in the mind of a ruthless child,
slowly pulling the legs off a spider,
ripping the wings off a butterfly,
and nonchalantly wiping away the color
that stains his precious fingers,
the knife is my crucifix
my soul pleads for someone else,
something else, to bare this,
the hurt bleeds out of my eyes,

and cries to the warmth of my pillow,
every tear that falls tonight,
is shed for you.
every scream my heart cuts
into the muted abyss of night be
echos from me to you.
every pitiful gasp for air,
is me breathing in the memory of you.
and your memory of me,
will grant us a meeting place,
somewhere between the fallen moon,
and the rising sun.

Extinction of a Home — Sept. 7, '03

I used to smile,
without a heavy heart tugging downwards
on the corners of my mouth.
I used to laugh,
because life was enveloped
in your sunshine.
Everything was so pure,
untainted and innocent,
unaware of its dirty future.
White is the easiest to stain.
We used to play,
childhood games late into the night,
deaf to the ticking away of time.
We took for granted,
the eutopia we had

and now all we have is the memory.
I used to be content,
with every aspect of my life,
until it was ripped away...
Time deteriorates.
So now im stuck,
longing for what is no more,
i can never have it back.
Not one more day,
no second chance fairytales,
just a hole in my heart,
clawing at weakness,
in hopes of escaping reality,
and alleviating the sickening pain,
change is uncurable.

So you ache for home,
But what exactly does that mean?
What is it to be homesick?
To tearfully awake every morning,
with your insides in a knot,
only untied by familiarity.
Familiarity,
that you'll never find again,
because it doesn't exist anymore.
Am I condemned to feel like this forever?

FALTERING

Nov. 3 '03

Am I supposed to be capable of handling this?

Am I supposed to be fine?

Leaden brick after another,

until my shoulders collapse,

and puncture my lungs in a gross miscalculation

I can't breathe.

Am I supposed to smile now?

Is this my cue to laugh?

I can't find it, it's lost somewhere,

if I search hard enough I'll be lost too,

in the darkness, like a gaping mouth,

hungry for my soul.

Was someone supposed to have been here?

Was I supposed to bleed to them?

Leave the blanket here over my insides,

they're dead and no one should behold them,
they only care because im fading,
and they need my light to see,
I guess these sounds your uttering,
should mean something,
but I cant hear you, I dont understand
and I know you cant fathom me.
Am I supposed to crawl out this window?
Is this the escape you provided me?
Im eight stories from the ground
trapped in a burning reverie,
clouded visions blind my eyes,
a year of drought + short comings.

VOID

Twisting, turning, ever seeking,
nothing.
Stretching, burning, ever reaching,
empty space.
Desiring, yearning, for some understanding,
denied.
Gasping, choking, on the truth,
is accepting that there is none.

CANVAS

11/17/03

Once again it was too much to contain,
I let it loose in a steady flow
of crimson rain.
Once again I was on the floor,
broken in a pathetic heap,
crying behind the safety of a locked door.
I loathe to be a burden for you to bare,
to shame and disgrace,
to grasp your heart and rip and tear.
I loathe this descention into despair,
this aching, throbbing, hopelessness,
dropping me into hell & leaving me there.
So to spare you from all of this,
I plaster this smile, this masquerade,
not a hint that something is amiss.

FOREIGNER

11/17/02

A lone figure clad in black,
heavily trudging,
each movement painstakingly weaking,
each heart beat begrudging,
breathing contempt into the face of night,
defiant, provoking,
slowly indulging the hot springs.
they brim and spill evoking,
nothing more than denial,
a brisk swipe of the hand,
fleeting courage, fleeting hope,
a stranger in a foriegn land.

HOMECOMING
11/24/03

Finally I can breath again,
Finally I can feel,
Consuming desire for every beat,
I can't believe this is real...
My mind is swimming,
In a sea of anguished doubt,
has hope been concieved in the shadow?
have I truely been given a way out?
conceived in an intoxicating cloud,
floating through minutes, hours, days,
unable to grasp it, to comprehend,
lost in some intangible haze,
Like the rising sun,
penetrating, piercing the night,
My burden is lifted,

my shoulders are light.
Dont take this away,
Dont let this die,
This hope is my lifesupport,
If its dead, so au I.

RE-BIRTH   12/4/03

Fear. Overwhelming doubt.

Searching, frantcly for expiration dates,

to mark the end of this newly purchased life,

when the light will run out.

Tremors. Of hope, come and go.

Grasping, with all I am,

with the desperate strength of despair,

lest I slip from life and fall below.

Running. Chasing, glimpses of a smile,

persuing shadows as fast as my heart will beat,

until my lungs explode.

to convince this eutopian dream to last a while.

Climbing. A burning rope.

Scaling cliffsides to safety,

Weary, pulling myself up, plagued w/ lathargy,

bruised, bloody, and broke.
Thriving. Swimming, in a foggy haze.
Uncertain, yet boldly daring,
to wold this new world,
trusting, in the promise of better days.

Futile Persuits

12/9/03

How many have trampled,
the grass on both sides,
and shattered, found,
niether ushered to their intense needs,
niether flourished, nor embellished care,
void of beauty, entangled in weeds,
vast wastelands of usage-filled disdain,
withered, puckered, dying,
yet boastfully claiming independence from the rain.

GOODBYE   12/31/03

I dont know how to walk away from you,
words that refuse to part from my lips.
goodbye.
tearing from my insides,
a shudder, a violent tremor of remorse,
no.
this is not allowed, these tears are taboo
how dare you disappoint them again,
protect.
dont pierce their precious little hearts,
theyre crying for you,
guilt.
quick, wipe your eyes and smile,
I think they believe youre fine,
decieve.

to willfully mislead the enemys,
liar, murder, protecter, are you kind?
foe?
but they love you, why are you pulling?
confusion, swimming, spiraling out of control,
drunk. .
with confusion that overwhelms,
w deranding in my head,
heart.
is torn in half but it's not fair,
split between oceans vast and sprawling,
bleeding.
for you, for them, for me?
can we wash this all away?
white out.

a favorable 'blink',
you're supposed to know what to do,
perfect.
but there is no such thing,
because it is merely relevant
truth,
must be universal and unchanging,
so here i am still rusty
frozen,
to the place where i left you,
where the words broke my heart,
goodbye.

- POISON -

12/31/03

Our bodys pressed tight
bonded in one last embrace,
an unfeeling farewell in an unfeeling night
We can not find the tears to shed,
or the words to speak,
they're lost in the chaos in our heads.
One month ago you moved away,
only we were still together,
until my flight today.
I will not resent, i will not blame you
for your calloused heart,
sometimes thats the only way to continue
...But i will keep feeling,
even if it kills me,
because apathy is not living.

Bonds of FREEDOM

1:45 AM
2/21/09

Came to me in the middle of the night

on a surge of tears

overflowing from my heart

destroy me.

Searing through the layers

sinking your teeth in

bath them in my inadequacies

blood letting.

the color neatly decorates

draws an intricate design

a portrayal of truth

epitome of reflection.

Learn to bare the marks

these are your cure-all

these are honest

these are chains.

KODAK?

2/21/09

To take a picture
to capture this moment
and suffocate it in plastic
to leave my sorrow
my heavy-leaden heart
with a splintered encasement
to display it for the world
set upon a shelf
apart from all normalcy
mock and stare
I can't move in here.

TUESDAY
MARCH 2nd '04

* Copeland @ THE SOCIAL
w/ Mae, The Working Title & Slow Day Coming
* Justin → saw Tallie → trashy taco bell
(home 11:45 ....yessss!!)
Got PIC WITH AARON MARSH!!
slap bracelet   COPELAND SHIRT

:)
sam

I LOVE COPELAND.

Mom & Dad   4/6/04

I open my mouth & the words wont come
out, they're buried somewhere inside me,
a vast graveyard that lies unmarked & readily
forgotten. Id rather forget. You'd be better
off behind that blindfold, I dont want you
to see. I dont want to hurt you. Im broken
& this flight parallels all we wish we could
leave behind.... but it will catch us. I cant
run fast enough, & endurance is lacking. Im
void of the defiance required to fight this
off, im so drained by the constant facade.
Yet, i could never collapse into you, i could
never stop. I wouldnt know how to end this.
Im so sorry. Im sorry for all the pain,
the disappointment, the lies, the shame, for

bieng the dirt under the rug. Sweep aside all the complications of my life so that it appears presentable. I know you never meant it like that. I never meant to be this way, but you dont even know it. Its a whole different world that lies undiscovered by you, : I prefer to keep it that way. I dont think you'd understand, : I dont want your sympathy. I dont want to be the little child in your arms, Id rather cry alone.... and I dont know why. These tears are ungrateful, are they not selfish? Are they not wrong? What more is there, whats left? I dont want to do this, I just want to forget. To erase the blur that leads up to here, thats all it is after all. A dark blue that plagues my memory & my heart. I love you, ... and so i cant tell you, I wont tell you. Im sorrys.

to tell or not to tell,
that is the
que stion

it doesn't seem fair
that your thousands of miles away,
and to think it's my fault,
that it was my weakness,
which caused us not to stay.
I wish I were stronger,
I wish i could have held on,
I never thought I'd want to be back,
that I could miss it so bad,
but it's forever gone.
I miss your true friendship,
I miss the depth of your care,
I want you back in my life,
I need you,
but you aren't there.

— April 26th 2004 —

○ The AKA's
○ Emery
○ Anatomy of a Ghost
○ The Beautiful Mistake

6:00 → 9:45(ish)pm @ the social
~ Savannah hated it!!!!! !!! ~

WE LOCKED OUR KEYS IN
      THE FLIPPN CAR!!
...³ we missed our exit...
... I was 4ouin. late getting home ....

Weeee ♥!

Eyes

We stand together, eyes averted
telescopes to magnify our insides
lethal weapons entrusted to no one
dormant. caged.
ugly.
We wouldn't dare to penetrate
we couldn't handle what we'd see
and there's no backtracking
Regret. mislead.
disappointed.
So we keep the barriers strong
we protect the truth
with hope, to even hide it from ourselves
forget. bury.
burning bridges.

Its the weakness in our armor
pathway straight to the heart
they must be gaurded
skeptic. tense.
privledged.
Will I let you gaze
deep inside of me
to x-ray every particle....
doors are locked for a reason.
walls are built with purpose
keep things in
keep things out
my eyes are shut.
.... but so are yours.

MIRROR   5/26/09

Pictures lay face down
spilling mournful stories
of friendships long decayed
unbeknownced to her.
The ties were stretched
over oceans
over years
maybe it hurt too much to see them break.
But now the truth
resonates with the sound
of crashing picture frames
and burning tears.
Clutching her knees to her chest
to keep her heart from falling out
she rocks back and forth

numb and swollen inside.
The debris
smoldering in the wake of her pain
a perfect reflection
a startling glance in the mirror.
And then the rain falls
intermingling with the blood on her arm
washing over her
it seems to cry
"I'm sorry"
and the remnants drift away.

YOU THOUGHT YOU WERE SO SMART
THE WAY YOU RAN & HID
FROM THE LIES THEY FED
FROM THE LIGHT THEY SHED
YOU WOULDN'T KNOW THE DIFFERENCE
CAUSE YOUR NOT LOOKING ANYWAY
MERELY RUNNING AS FAST AS YOUR HEART BEATS
DROWNING OUT THE SOUND W/ YOUR CRIES
AND AS YOU FAIL TO STOP TIME
AND THE SECOND HAND SLAPS YOUR FACE
ITS TOO LATE TO LISTEN
B/C YOU LEFT THE VOICES FAR BEHIND
ALONG W/ HOPE & PURPOSE
SO YOU FALL INTO THE VOID
THE DARKNESS ENVELOPES YOU

AND THERES NO JOY IN SKIES OF BLUE

NO BEAUTY LEFT TO FIND

YOU LEFT IT ALL BEHIND

YOU DONT THINK YOU'RE SO SMART ANYMORE

NOONE EVER SAID YOU COULDNT GO BACK.

** TRANSPARENT **

You read me
the story marked out so clearly on my wrist
your prying eyes devour every scar
burning through my skin
the shame you taught me
each time your thoughtless words stung my face
i hate you
the deproving expression dominating your features
as you declare me flawed
as you trample myself under your feet
the confidence in your charade
id rather bare these marks
rather be honest
your contradictions turn my stomach
and your eyes betray your dirty insides

I can see them seeping through
not much longer now
in not much longer you'll break too.

1:30 am   ...OOPS...   6/1/04

I cant keep my hand from shaking
so it enacts the shameful deed
I cant stop
Ive lost myself in the pain
and somehow i dont feel
as the blood splatters my sheet
and drips off my arm
I cant help but feel this is right
i only think it is wrong
but i dont want this
What will they say
what will they do
I will disappoint
and hurt
and shame

oh GOD IT HURTS SO BAD
my heart seems as though
it will explode
and thats just whats on the inside
what the fuck have I done
im so stupid, im so stupid
didnt you stop to think?
No, I only felt
I didnt want to feel
but you pushed me to the
END.
where are you in this
I bet you cant even look at me
this pathetic mess
of blood and tears

a shriveling, sobbing heap
collapsed on the floor
sneaking in the dark
to return the vessel
washed and dried
they'll never notice
im so pathetic
i dont know what to do
wont someone help
can something help?
i'll pay - and you know it,
i dont care anymore
shit.
.... help me out of this.
someone please, .. im so alone.

no one feels this
no one speaks
and neither do I
no one wants to
its a secret
    cssshhh!
dont spill your guts here
we dont want to clean them up
keep them baked inside
keep them locked inside,
its a lose, lose situation here.

HELP ME.

I watch with blurry vision
through eyes that swim in salty tears
as the blood sprawls across my wrist
and dives to caress, taint my sheets
bearing witness to the release of painful years.
the blade flashes in the night
it seems to smile as it sinks deep into my skin
donning triumphant lipstick on its mouth
to display its fulfillment of some glorified purpose
i close my eyes afraid to let reality set in.
what will they say of these marks?
will they overlook my final stand?
My last attempt to express
and try to separate the symbol from its meaning
I need you to take the knife out of my hand

6/22/01

You touched what wasn't yours to touch.
your devilish scheming
your lustful heart
shot forth limbs
well aquainted with self-serving,
calloused to ethics or human value.
they sprouted in me
choking out the life
tainting, poisoning,
stealing, degrading
violating, maiming my heart,
but i wont allow you to reside there
i wont grant permanence to my condition
I WILL FORGIVE YOU.

Wed., JUNE 23rd 2004 ..... @ the social

    DEad PoEtIC
*   HASte the DAY
    ANother broken promise
*   DEmoN HUNteR
Went with ███████, 711→FRaPPacinos
100.3 Sing ALongs !! → My House

.... Who is this?!.....
- FiNch?- ...no... -huu...-
- the CACA PENIS'S?! -
  ... WHAT?! ....

.... she's one of Jamie's Friends ....
- I know she was no good -
"███ Your A JUSTIFIABLE ASSHOLE"

to exist
to reside, forever after
in their minds and hearts
to impact their lives
with the legacy of ours
to flee
to scatter, as diminishing shadows
or to stay, as favorable memories
the choice is ours
and ours alone.

6/28/04

I fold myself into boxes
filtering out the pieces I no longer like
reminiscent of the past
and hopeful for the future
as naked walls stand gawking.
A sterile poison takes up residency
with outstretched arms
and gaping mouth
threatening to swallow me whole
as I dutifully feed it space.
happless strangers
yearning for new acquaintances
to acquire new stories
praying for permanence
as the ones that wait for me

July 8, 2004 @ Wills Pub

(■■■■)

THE ROCKET SUMMER

(and.... who cares...)

SICK

WHY?

pointed fingers

TEARS

SCABS

BLOOD

clarity

hurt

KNIVES

DEATH of LOVE

DISAPPOINTMENT

empty spaces

SHOES

ME WITHOUT YOU

THE WORKING TITLE

*** Love Drug *** July 11th, 2004
Noise Ratchet   (5am)

- THE SOCIAL -

█████ Noah & Jean Francis

- FREAK'N AWESOME SHOW!!!! -

* ALMOST died in a car crash
on the way home~ ALWAYS wear
a flippin seatbelt!! sheezah....

You said love

& like an ocean wave slapping your face
the word crashed into me
knocking me down
you told me i could never disappoint you
how did you come to feel this way
about the pathetic mess that is me
where is the beauty you describe
i cant comprehend
but i love the feel of your words
as they caress my heart
as they pray on my behalf
and ease this pain
.... you said love.

THE QUESTION

to eat, or not to eat

that is the question

and we stumble over it every day

under the guise of 'all-together'.

some nondescript add

spews poison into our brains

'repeat all'

and its perpetual haunting stings your face

cements your teeth

your not hungry anyway

the mirror told you so

then it wrapped your image

securely around your memory

in order to deflect any other comments

and keep intruders away

protect them from "it"
you dont want to disappoint
hide away until you can fix it
flat like its supposed to be
presentable and perfect
just like they want it
the customer is always right.

(thanks for the nudge in the right direction)
Ryan....

— A PRAYER —   1:30 am

I hurt everywhere, and no where all at
once. I feel so disillusioned, yet its
catalyst was clarity. Reality shifted
through the cracks, a rude awakening.
Why would You give me these dreams?
You compare yourself to a parent → if
your child asked for food you would
not give him a stone, these dreams
are outstretched arms reaching as the
child to it's father, feed my soul. Im
sorry. Im sorry for my failures, for
my doubts, help me not to put you in
a box. Mend me, use me, I am yours.
Thank you for always persuing me, even
when I turn my back & run away. You're

incredible. I take you for granted, I'm
so sorry. Father, Friend, Shepard, Pursuer
of my soul, HEALER, Light. Thank you.
I love you.

ПОШОЛ НАХОЙ
(НИКИТА)
-Nick-

These songs run through my perritory
playing pictures
of you and me
I feel your breath against my skin
your arms around my waist
as you turn the key; let us in
the receding chill of the winter night
I can taste the cocktails
and you dim the light
your lips against mine
the swell of your cologne
caus me to lose track of time
I never wanted to leave your embrace
though it was empty
it was an escape from that place

→

I can hear you speak
your Russian accent
overwhelms me ; I feel weak
and as the cd plays
I sit here missing you
and those winter days.

My feet hit the pavement
but i dont feel
Im Running, leaving it all behind
the tears
mingle with the sweat on my face
quick friends, they plunge to the ground
a sob escapes my lips
its drownd by the roar of my thoughts
keep Running
my lungs are burning
head spinning
yet each step brings clarity
the night is welcoming
its mine
there is no one to rob me of this

for once everything is as it seems
I trust this
street lights flicker on
their images smear across the water
creating a nightmarish spectacle
and I revel in its beauty
it's dark & loneliness
misunderstood, feared
and it's me
a curve in the road
shadows reach to envelope me
I cant feel my legs
but I keep moving, I cant stop
the sweat glistens on my arms
I can taste it on my lips

my breath, in beats of four
is the music
my eyes are fixed ahead
some undetermined goal
nothing matters anymore
I left it all behind
lost in this late night run

HIDE
PENANCE
ripped art.
uneasy
LIES
microscope
BURDEN
Weak
chaos
SCABS
my favorite knife
GRIEVE
TOO LATE.
darkness
release
sulets
bloodshed
PAIN
alone
locked doors
Blind
SPINNING
LOSS
TRANCE
tears
HELP.
dull ache
a FAILURE
a FALL
a MEANS TO AN END
...THATS ALL.
pathetic
NUMB
fragile
cover of darkness
VOICES IN my head
a letter
what the fuck is WRONG with ME?
irrevocable

These marks are made in your honor tonight

although you dont deserve to be here

caught off-gaured

I shed a tear

I bled your name

alone in my fortress grieving

for times long gone

scabs ripped off before healing

and iu not sure where to go from here

funny iu the only one to care

you cleared your conscience

with a letter that you left there

I cant let you back in.

...and so we walk, hand in hand, heart in hand.

CARE

Support

Time

WHAT DO YOU SEE HERE?!
— It must not be ue... —

disappoint

TRUST (2.)

I WANT YOU. (so bad)
SO I SHOULD LET YOU GO.
— im scared —

IM HANGING ON YOUR WORDS
(or are they hanging ues?)

listen

hurt

(and still I tell you...)

comfort.

GLANCE BACK (at a picture) 8/27/09

That girl, shes dead

I dont know how I lost her

I dont know where she went

please dont ask for her anymore

a busy signal

a disconnected line

like a friend who moved away

that you lost touch with

"no forward adress available"

I think i miss her

but who was she anyway?

and who am I...

♡ THE WORKING TITLE ♡

London is Tonight

- SMOKE BREAK! - (2.)

@ Wills Pub

~ Justin, Luke and John ~

saw Ryan, Richie, Kelly, Courtney [3] Danielle

Crazy Car Wars !! ★

(beloved Taco Bell)

..."OH, ITS A UNISEX
BATHROOM..."

"you were so brave; bold Renee"

shirt
bitch

Tommy's monologe in the bathroom
(audience: one perturbed child)

Potty breaks
for John

BURN THEM W/ YOUR
CIGARETTE!!

The darkness closes in
a free consuming oxygen
hands reach towards the light
perpetual searching
continual fight
all for nought.
Spinning mercilessly
uncontrolable shivers ravage my body
something soft to soothe
to take the chaos
I cant move
and the words are frozen.
Weighted heavily
poignant, icy
stuck in a world inside my head

severed ties to the outside
something that you said
Its drownding me.

-PM-

these pills go down so softly

see, there's nothing too it

isnt this familiar?

isnt this so easy?

Oh my friend, you've been here before

you know how it goes

close your eyes

let the magic work

you know how it does

Dont be afraid, i locked the door

the evidence concealed

youre so smart

youre so stupid

hide until youre healed

⟨LEAGUE⟩

IN PASSING

I love RORY - J/K!!

@ WILLS PUB w/ GRANTUTH

~ Spent over two hours FINDING it, then missed RORY, what a crock! ~

...dont leave the table till youve smoked everything in the box.....

"guest list for 7/15/thing..." ███ at fairevella (sp?.)

~ DRANK ~

(n be tattoo)

"well throw our own damn show!!"

9/4/04

You look out at me from your post
on my guitar case,
and i can feel your hands on my wrist
lovingly they trace,
every line that resides so shamefully
but you dont shrink away,
my insides recoil at the thought
yet somehow you choose to stay,
You squeeze my hand as i speak the words
to tell the story of that night,
your eyes lock with mine so securely
and hold them tight,
they seem to be communicating with me
telling me it'll all work out,
and with each soothing stroke
i release my doubt.

Neva Dinova   10/8/04

** Vostok

** <u>THE GOOD LIFE</u> **

@ THE Social

Went with: Grant, Katie & Lexy

TIM KASHER IS SO= Hott!!
            xoxo   (can i take you home?!)

~ mocha frappacino's, cloves,
    and the wind in my face ~

6'9 Giant and 3 girls in a photobooth
        (GOOD JOB)

* Emery *   10/10/04

** FROM FIRST TO LAST **

Brazil ...goodbye sniper... coca.. boo

@ The social

went with: Grant, ████████ ; Danielle

"I want to have 'Sonny's' babies..."

████████

- YOU BURNT MY ARM! -   Kelly ; Courtney

27N, ███████████ FIRST SHOW

yes

...it was my
fault...

Richie

the ride home

Christina

A Letter of Sorts

To Someone Grand and i am no one, just one
and only all alone to think this through.
Just one, and many vultures circling in my head
is spinning, drowning from the weight
and i dont know what to do.
Choose your nightmare, i live mine and leave it
but its looming up ahead of me like a shadow
that i cast, and shattered glass
i threw the rock that was my inconsideration
caused you pain cause i succumbed to me so fast.
And fast they fall, they drop and plunge
plummet to their material graves
i watch them, feel them, hear their patter
create pitiful lakes
lakes of stain of evidenc that i feel... dont tell me
            its not my fault.

Someone murdered spring
She lies frozen and helpless
Under an ice veil.

Haiku
-colors-

-BLACK-

Dark, chaotic dreams
escaping and tainting life
An open coffin

-Red-

valiant beating heart
fighting against the silence
hanging by a thread

-Grey-

shadowy unknown
calloused shield of protection
apathy is death

-White-

a falling snowflake
resemblance of all thats pure
easiest to stain

I WANT TO GET AWAY FROM YOU
I WANT TO GET AWAY FROM ME
I WANT TO RIP MY HEART OUT
AND NUMBLY WATCH IT BLEED.
I WANT TO GET AWAY FROM YOU
I WANT TO GET AWAY FROM ME
I WANT TO TEAR A WHOLE IN MY THROAT
SO YOU CAN HEAR ME SCREAM.

A STORM

Vibrant colors painted the sky

a masterful illusion so intriguing that I

briefly succumbed to its story

and hopeful let it in

only to discover it was tainted

as the canopy grew dim

It was a dark and brooding dance

as light struggled for a chance

yet clumsily blown aside

by a stronger, determined gale

I watched and felt it overpower

Inside me ever so frail.

A violent arousal stirring change

a spectrum of life and death arrange

spinning in chaotic whirlwinds ⟹

ushering away the past
while onlookers implore to have it back
the darkness snuck in so fast.
A memory forcibly holds it writhing
like thunder chasing lightening
as worlds fall apart to the song of the wind
that brilliant portrait is forever gone
in emerging newborn dream buds her knell
so long, fair sky, so long.

I WASN'T GOOD ENOUGH

YOU HAD SOMETHING ON THE SIDE

ALL I HAD TO OFFER WAS MY HEART

YOU HAD NO USE FOR THAT

NOT WHEN SHE LET YOU INSIDE

YOU CARED NOT FOR MY POETRY

AND NOTHING OF MY SONG

YOU SOUGHT TO FULFILL

YOUR SELFISH DESIRES

STRINGING ME ALONG

I STAYED BESIDE YOU

ALL THE WHILE YOU DID DRINK

AND ANGRILY YOU'D RETURN

AN AGENDA AND A FIST

AND I'D JUST LET YOU HIT ME

→

SOONER OR LATER I CAME TO REALIZE

THAT MAYBE THIS WASNT OK

MAYBE I DIDNT DESERVE THIS

MAYBE I SHOULD SUFFICE

SO I TOOK BACK MY HEART AND FADED AWAY.

It wasn't supposed to be this way
it faded too quickly
like a fucking nicotine high
a shitty ride at the park
they have the nerve to point at you
and say it was your fault
for expecting so much out of life
this anticlimactic story
to droning on
drilling holes into my head
so much potential
never reached
dreams caged in jars
never released
and its your fault they suffocated

youre to blame
for all of these inadequacies
these cheap generic aspirations
a fucking Goodwill of futures
pick through the leftovers
of yesterdays inhibitions,

THE REASONS

I tore your heart

so tear my flesh

slice the cells apart

bleeding for you

is all I know to do

as I lay here on the floor.

turmoil and torment

torturous treason and tearful goodbyes

the poisonous regrets

that infect our eyes

an eye for an eye

heart for a heart

and descending I

depart

determined to die

Senses Fail

three

Name Taken   HOB   (Bah, what
              10/15/04   a crock)
Silverstein   ...they all sucked...

* GRANT, ████████████, katie, Courtney

Daniel...

the "smoking porch"   TRAFFIC   Scarf
(WT?!?)   DEADLY KISSES

tired as hell   "THAT'S NOT
                                           FUCKING COURTNEY!!"

"she saw me kissing   SLEEP CHAIN
you so she left..."

"...but fucking A
I didn't know that
would suck that much"

MR. HAZZAS BAND @ HOB

w/ Grant, ███████████ (21, haha)

can I interest
you in a purple hooter?!

"   CLOVES

Sex on the beach

RED HEADED SLUT

"OH. THEY'RE NOT PLAYING TONIGHT"
- LIAR -

10/31/04

the words you speak are so sweet
but they're starving me
caught in the middle
torn apart
I just want to be with you
I just want to trust
I want you to be here
when i open my eyes
burn these lies
this blood is yours
you are the knife that cuts
Im screaming inside this cage
let me out so you can hold me
I want to feel you
and know this is true.

★ ★ ★ COPELAND ★ ★ ★   11/9/04

★ ★ Sparta ★ ★

★ further seems forever ★

Sunshine (sucked)

@ HOB - day after my b-day

my Grant and ██████

touch me   ♡ them

crazy   "you know I like you
smoking porch   Hot Right!"

"██████ better..."

SHITTY RIDE

HOME

California

Pineless   Black & Mild

11/1/09

Sometimes I wish we could all just let go
  and rise, like this smoke
above all the greys that cloud this world
away with the wind, toss and twirl
away with the wind to another world
we'd leave this all behind & breath again
we'd leave this all behind and then
the dirt would crumble, fall from the frame
and leave a picture so pure and beautiful
beholding this eutopia we'd be changed
no, we'd never be the same...

Camping

Intoxicated,
drunk from your kiss
your potent words
and this bottle
under a sky, winking stars
under a blanket, blinking hard
your lips on my neck
you feel so good
hold me
your arms, wrapped secure
your promises, I rest assured
you won't hurt me
All I have to fear
is myself, and I am
vulnerable.

soccer?

Community Service

ALCOHOLIC

GROUNDED FOR
- TWO MONTHS -

LIAR

What will your sister
think of you now?

"I wanted to believe every lie you
ever told me ..."

can I hug you?

you're
such a
good actress

disappointed

I
WILL
HOSPITALIZE
YOU

ITS
your
FAULT
we're
here

(we don't want to be here)

LIAR

We're so

are you
going to
cut
YOURSELF?

college?

(promise me you
won't)

CAR?

I don't deserve to have anyone
touch me.

✶ ✶ I've been having panic attacks
at school, and the safe-officer
threatened to Baker Act me.
My dad mentioned hospitalizing
me to keep me from cutting.
My head and body was
shaking uncontrollably, their
voices were screaming inside
of my head on repeat. It's
turned into a horrible
nightmare. Please don't let
anyone take me away. I'm
supposed to see a psychiatrist.
The latest are scissors and a
butter knife from Panera.

To Dad   12/19/04

She spreads her paper wings
They unfold in vibrant majesty
The wind feels blessed beneath her sails
A symbol of the beautiful things,
She lifts and gently floats away
Her flight parallels the falling plastic
Shimmers of colored dust drip in excess
I watched her sparkle amongst the days,
The caterpillar forever changed
All traces of her ugly past removed
She is a new creation
The cocoon lies estranged,
And soft, she ascends into night's embrace
winking at the stars
The moon smiles fondly down upon her
The epitome of savory grace.

Twenty signatures, twenty lies
twenty times
I stared into your vacant eyes
Black holes, black lights
black fights
And sleepless nights
You pulled the trigger
Shot forth from the guitar strings
I watch them, played like me
feel myself slipping
Burnt like my pictures
and torn
Hatred comes so easily
To think I believed you were mine,
But I shared you twenty times.

IVE GOT YOU PINNED
AGAINST THE WALL
YOUR HEART SHOULD
BE POUNDING
BUT I HEAR NOTHING
AT ALL.

4/05

Heavy, frozen layers, blocks of ice.
calloused, unreachable — open your
fucking mouth and SAY SOMETHING...
but I cant   I dont know where the
words are —   a pencil in my head
where they should be   damn I
need a cigarette ... fag...(who the
fuck calls it that?! Youre such a
freako weirdo) Walking down the
aisle in Target pressing all the "try
me!" buttons, chaos — press record,
play — repeat all, level eight (or is
it louder? God, stop screaming I
cant think) — who wants to think
anyways   a line of yellow tape

CRIME SCENE INVESTIGATION - NO
TRESSPASSING ... "Can I hug you?"
meltdown, warning - it swallowed
contact poison control immediately
I am poison. I destroy all I touch,
Rogue on X-men Im draing your
energy (Can you hear me? Are you
that magical?) - I havent said
anything   SPEAK UP   weights
chained to words drowning inside
of me God Im so sorry, Im
so sorry   dagger, dagger, dagger
dagger (will you ever stop stabbing
them? YOU ARE HURTING EVERYONE)
Bitch, here - show her a MIRROR

You dont deserve to be touched, I dont want anyone to touch me I want someone to touch me what the fuck do I want? I dont know, I dont know Pussy marks you pussy ass bitch, couldnt you do any better than that? Oh, thats too messy Look at him, hes crying ITS YOUR FAULT look what you did you stupid bitch How COULD YOU DO THAT TO ME? You said just fifteen minutes. I was never in the picture. How DARE YOU?! We never discussed this oug I cant breath ... yes you can, you can ... where are those words I ordered last week?

Open the door!" Open the door!!. (fuck
NO) You picked it open, you always
do, pry it open.. tsch, nosey nosey...
what the hell is privacy anyway?
Dont ask me, my door wont shut
now. (assholes) ANIMAL IN A CAGE
- go ahead, point, stare, discuss me
and my habits I wouldnt understand -
flicker hints of flame snuffed
out every time I CANT GET THE
FUCKING FLAME TO STAY i hate
this piece of shit lighter I hate
it I HATE IT. fuck. Your
crazy. Now. about those guitar
lessons ... play your heart out.
(I want to play my heart out)

A ride at the fair, spinning flashing blurring lights and noise. I'm dizzy. "Do you want to throw up?" God no, that's disgusting. fruit salad. cucumber - just three days, look at us!! Guui. You can use my toothbrush" How could you do THAT TO ME? The longer you go the harder it is. I'm sorry, I'm so sorry I couldn't there were too many - filter. A tingling, burning sensation in my nose eyes are drowning (stop crying.) Houdini. Please just make it all disappear. Just make it all go away. Oh hey, there's black all down your face!!"

holy fuck!! I didnt know that....
label it 'poison' in big black ink
letters, read it: P-O-I-S-O-N
One injection of apathy, coming right
up - oh, u sorry there appears to
be a shortage - NUMB. The kind of
crying where you cant see and youre
head throbs and your heart ACHES
(scrutinize the word, feel it) and
you feel dead Something soft
please "Take this weight away" - thank
you Connor Oberst. GOD, I love
Bright Eyes. what the hell is wrong
with you? FEB 5TH - assholes,
ASSHOLES (so are you) I know you
dont understand - OK, take it out,

Ive had ENOUGH!!   —or we? (are you
sure youre not talking about wo?)
fuck up. fuck up. FUCKED UP.
fuck up. I know, IM sorry
but what good is that anyway
How bout another five months, hell
your grounded teou graduation....
I cant eat I cant sleep   to
sleep perchance to dream   what
dreams may come — I dont want to
find out it all just hurts so bad
check the TV guide whats next
on the boob tube (who the fuck
calls it that?!) "when everything
feels like the movies yeah you bleed
just to know youre alive" humm.

Rewind - no, fast forward, "when
everything went to be BROKEN, I
just want you to know who I am "
Why?! fidget. I'll get you up
in time for breakfast - no. I dont
want any. Want ue to make you
something for lunch? No. not hungry.
(YES!!) What do you want for
dinner? NOTHING. (tears, shut up,
stop crying bitch) 20 signatures?!
I dont care I hate you. Glass walls
soundproof Rooms I can see them I
can never change the porcelain faces
melt the frozen hearts hooks
YANK different directions
Abort mission. give up. your friends suck

A butterfly tattoo. why dont you just say something? I CANT I cant find them anywhere "Now Renee, dont grind your teeth" 1:30 one plus three is four and zero makes fourty. Three minus one is two plus zero is still two, or add on zero is twenty. Reduce to items, extract meaning, anihilate zero and there are two items, spread evenly across, divided by two dots (or a neutral line) 11-(which is two) 8-86, great birth date. "Im sorry im not emotionally available" - she has baggage Are you familiar with the Baker Act? A plastic butter knife from Panera

scissors

My dads (siccors) (how the hell is that spelled?!) Butcher knife a piece of glass a razor how pathetic allways even number 2, 4, 6, 12, 16, 18 never more than that (psycho) blood letting, pennance release distraction ('why? we dont understand') Red for blood and blue for tears 'The past when you choose to let it be that' - the NERVE. Im so LOST (Wed. night at eight, we'll have to record) Please make this stop. ... How dare you...

I LIKE IT A LOT! ITS
REALLY GOOD!

1/30/05

"Beautiful" she tells me "absolutely
gorgeous" and he once told her he
thought me an angel, I snicker gag
who was he looking at? The tree tops
dance, haunting shadows of men
swaying menacingly back and forth on
the roof tops (hats off to you, you're
so sneaky) Millions of predators lurk
outside these doors and I wonder which
one shall ensnare me next, what line
will it be? I'm confident I've heard
them all ... but they are always scheming.
Please just lock me away this is
getting the best of me — it's so lonely —
NO, I wouldn't flatter myself to think
I'm the only one to suffer, but

We suffer seperate, solitary, slipping
past surveillance, company, help. We
silently endure inside ourselves and
no one is there but 'I'. And once
in a while we touch in chords
strung together in a melody, beating
together in break downs, but then
the moment comes to pass... it passes
and we're back inside the cells we
built (who built?) and I cant seem
to point a finger (anywhere but at
myself). So I slip back through the
window dim the lights and close
my eyes in the darkness.

THERE IS A DIFFERENCE
BETWEEN WHAT IS SAID

AND WHAT IS IMPLIED

WHILE YOUR WORDS KISS MY HAND
THE UNSPOKEN STABS MY HEART

AND THE TEARS ARE

DENIED

THESE FEELINGS ARE UNJUSTIFIED.

BRIGHT EYES

Neva Dinova
Jesse Sykes

FEB. 5th

Hoodie
Jason

Osbourn

"do you know how
to get there?"
-sure

- STARE DOWN -

"no!

Kelly

Posters

T-shirt

Smoking Porch

the crazy merch tips

Julia

EUROPEAN
RELATIONS

"friends hug goodbye!"

"How do you say it?" — Neh-vah Dinohva
"Neeeva Dinooovah?!" — AH! SILLY !!
DRUNK.

2/15/05

This spinning, it has a name
& had a face, a sticky note
a million labels on my forehead
Over analyze my every move
categorize, check it off on your list
observe the specimen in its cage
"A miracle you're alive"
It echoes in my head
then tears are loud
flickering light
the sounds are mixing
splurging together
screaming, and I can't hear
screaming, and I'm so far away

$\longrightarrow$

from that place
where they hunted out the spinning
gave it a name.
gave it a face

2/19/05

TASTE OF CHAOS TOUR

A Static Lullaby
Senses Fail
Killswitch Engage
Underoath
....NORA....

(mostly attracted)

"my left butt cheek
candy..."

bitch drinks

Katie   Ryan
Os

Jason

Nicole

GRANT

Goodwill shirts

Ralph's shirts

English
dude

Anthony

crosseyed sissy
cockdick

Amy Jace
Kylie

PARKING LOT
PARTY

DRUNKARDS

CHAPSTICK RESPECT !!

2/28/05

You sat there, you listened
listened to my tears
hit the phone
contemplating
the rhythm of my breaths
in... out... (stutter?)
as I sunck off
into sleep
still,
you remained there
taunted by my screams
on the floor
the anxious silence
when it fell to black
whispers

softly back to us
there   there.

———————— x x x ————————

And so this comes to a close
a premeditated 'end'
And its not the end
It will never go away
It will never leave me
and im left with one simple phrase
THIS IS ME.....

2/28/05

"eeten.....i mean..... aaGH!!"

The angels wings are torn
she's weeping on the shore
all alone, in the dark
grains of sand stand by
watching as she cries
* there is nothing left
there is nothing left
of the life she led
- her halo's broken by her side
and there's no reason to try
A hole is dug she crawls inside
ready and willing to die
all alone, in the dark
stars are screaming out of the sky
as the angel cries *
She softly closes tearful eyes
and lets the world slip by
all alone, in the dark
the footprints wash away
she's all that remains and *

→

Then someone came along
and gave her a new song
he sat with her, in the dark
he said he'd hold her forever
and never leave her side, now
* There is nothing left
There is nothing left
of the life she bled
And shes not alone anymore.

My mind it jumps
from here to there
and in between I
feel things when I please
then leave it somewhere
out of reach
they swing
or do I?
kick and pull or push
it is posed to me
perhaps
I am all of these
and it makes me spin.
I hate you I love you
come here go away
BRAKE ME
am I not shattered already?
and there isnt enough space
to tell you where I am

A scared little girl
who's teary wide eyes
observe the specimens
from beneath a striped hat
no one sees her
and everyone sees her
arms
black rivers down her cheeks
thoughts disrupted by
the crude woman in a pink blanket
belching and ~~disturbing~~ the silent halls
with her compulsive shouting
He is old and demented
he speaks of war
and the end of the world
he makes a gun with his fingers
and angrily points at the striped hat
"BANG!!"
His volatile stench combines
with his vicious cry

and He is incoherent, He is shitting on himself
screaming, shooting His gun
the observers in the glass case
come running with their needles,
their medicine, and they are hunters
they sedate the vile old man
and lock him away in a room
you can hear his shouts
reverberating in the sterile empty halls
plastic couches with barnacles
we are barnacles
attached to the plastic
there is no where to go
no escape
perhaps an empty corner
even there
safety alludes us.
(and this is safe..?)
shakes   tremors   screams of horror
and the drugs

give us our drugs
our new addiction
only escape
heavily medicated
they slump and nod their little heads
sitting in the chairs
smoking in our cage
and sitting in the chairs
the stripped hat 's crying
the pink blanket perches
begins to sing in spanish
a man in a wheel chair
with cuts on his legs
rants and raves
"this is a mistake! im not supposed to be here"
we know by the cuts on his legs.
and 72 hours pass by
and they wont let her go
and she is scared
the girl in the stripped hat

she is scared and alone
and then
a boy
brown hair and genuine eyes
soft and calm
to hold her hand
they shake   together
He sits with her
He is a knight (her knight)
come to hold her little hand
and the observers
seek to pervert their fairytale
they are the world
and we are removed
children hiding under tables
in a secret garden
crossing bridges to 'teribinthia'
He shares His cigarettes
promises to stay
and the stripped Hat is scared... but not
                                        alone

and they have come to let her go
and his big brown eyes are swimming
(click)
forever in her head
as she passes through the doors
away from the horror
back to her nightmare
shocked and numb
confused and traumatized
but she is free
and the hat is useless.

(REHAB)

Choose your nightmare   8/25/04
they say
as they sit comfortably in couches
Choose your nightmare
they say
as she cringes, cornered on pins and needles
And the little girl in her head is angry
whispering, loud   in her ear
Run away! Escape!
but she is glued to pins and needles
that prick tiny holes in her heart
they push
she pulls
until the tears in his eyes
become salt in her wounds
and she concedes
her cover is blown
there is no where to hide
no place left to mask the pain
and she tingles as the feeling returns

it haunts her
drives her faster towards the edge
Oh! to be numb!!
to be immune
from the pain in her body
to lock the monsters tight in a bottle
burn them into smoke
to be blown away in the stale night air
to run fast enough
and leave it all behind
but she is drained
there's a hole in her stomache
weights on her legs
they are catching her
and she begins to shake
sad, infront of strangers
far away
there are no secrets (and no where to hide)
and He is asking her to come home
and she's afraid

and He is begging her to come home
where she is safe
and she's afraid
this is all she knows
this is her hiding place
He holds her hand
as she shakes
closes her salty eyes
and takes a step
blind.

A twenty dollar bill   8/23/09
lies on the floor
I imagine it rolled up
dancing over snow
My mouth tingles
And she is drinking water
in a green bottle
It looks like beer (Heineken)
I can smell it   taste it....
I could snort
coffee beans
imagine it shooting straight into my brain
eyes dialate
I would steal
to get that high
I would sell (myself)
to escape
so desperate
so anxious
twitching

to feel
the blade against my wrists
yes, I would cut
to get that high
I would ~~entire~~ be ~~assess~~
a cowardly lion
and lie n(MANIPULATE) ~~him~~ him
to get what I need   (want?)
and I'm a bitch
and he is angry
crying in his truck
but I don't care
I have my favorite drugs
I would deceive
to get that high
this is my mirror
it does not lie
~~asss~~ (how ugly I am ~~and~~ inside....)
I saw, & began to cry
pushing me to go away

away to another 'holding cell'
(oh, its not just another holding cell, they say)
why waste another month in there
when you can rest, safe
in areas that wish to help you?
I crumble, I fall (reluctantly)
collapse into the promise
of better days
a purpose for the pain
and hope
(do I dare to hope?)
to return changed.

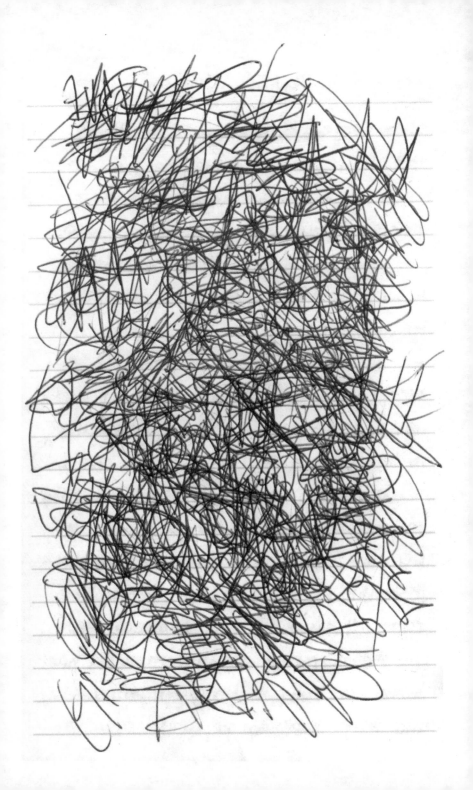

<u>BEFORE</u>　　　RELAPSE
　　　　　　　　　　　　　　　8/29/05

I am angry, humiliated, degraded and
alone. I feel like an animal back in the
hospital, it is overwhelming and I cant
breath. I am anxious and hurt, helpless,
powerless, and restless. I dont know what to
do with the way I feel. I dont want to
feel (like this) and my only coping
mechanisms have been taken from me. I
cant cut, I cant listen to music, I cant
call a friend and I cant go do something
to take my mind off of things.... and Im
so frustrated & angry I feel like a venomous
snake, a rabid dog foaming at the mouth.
My mind is racing in a million directions
it shouldnt go, a million dark corners I'd
rather not expose .... there is so much to
say and no one to say them to, and I hurt.
I hurt so badly I dont know what to do, I
just want it all to go away....

After

I am

so vile

so wretched, pathetic

I should be punished

punished for being a failure

(another failure, how fitting)

for disappointing   again....

clad in black

I wear my shame

for all to see

(and is this how they'll think of me?)

...but today I wear white

clean and pure

like my new slate

I will move forward

I will learn

I will not be poisoned by self hate

I am not the black sheep, or dirt under the rug

and I am loved.

The eyes stare   9/1/05
and they are *HIS*
burning holes deep into my body
scrutinizing every inch
HE lives inside of them
(the eyes)
and they are hurting me
they are
slits of glass
piercing my memory
greedy monsters
consuming my entire being
poisonous, lustful, perverted, fear
snaking it's way
to choke my heart
and I am swallowing stones
I am swallowing stones
I am alone
crying
there is no place to hide

#5 becomes *THEY*

and they awake

rudely

and rise from their graves

to haunt me

I shut my eyes

but his are still drilling

tormenting

stealing my breath

and I want to lash out

to remove the offenders

bury them somewhere far, far away

where they are blind

and can no longer touch me

but my arms have become putty

lay useless at my sides

I am mute

there's nothing

I

can do.

everything's a war   9/3/05
inside her head (heart)
And she is turning
to anything
that will stand in the place
of those she no longer has
she stuffs her mouth
to fill the hole
inside.
colors her lungs black
nails red
heart
is bleeding
onto her lips
distraught
overwhelmed
by fear
of whats to become of her
the shadows
lurk ahead

doom and gloom
heavy clouds
devour the sun
greedily swallowing
fragile hope
.... pleads, fights for life
there's not enough light
to sustain it
winter has come
taken up a permanent residence
lurking over her
mind explores
dark corners
knit tightly into cobwebs
filled with vicious secrets
writhing to be free
tangeling thouselves
in silky thread
that sticks
determined, to every word

nothing can save her

from

herself

the bellys of the clouds
give birth to
a thousand angry raindrops
that fall
hard
upon her heart
into her vulnerable eyes
(goddamn those eyes)
and perhaps everything's their fault
it is not a cleansing rain
this is a flood
intent on drowning her
she will sink
(or swim?)
and everythings a war inside her head.

I AM IN A WHITE ROOM
ALONE, WITH
BOTTLES AND BOTTLES OF LIQUOR
BEAUTIFUL POWDER MOUNTAINS
AND THE PILLS (OH! THE PILLS!)
THERE IS NO ONE HERE
to STOP ME
NO ONE
to SAVE ME
I AM dancing
RUNNING IN CIRCLES
I HAVE EVERYTHING I WANT
AND
I DONT KNOW WHERE to START
GRAB A BOTTLE
drAIN it
I AM FRANTIC
SHOVING MY FACE
INTO THE MOUNTAINS
CHEWING, SNORTING, HANDFULS OF PILLS LIKE CANDY

they pop into my mouth
like pez
i cant stop.
i dont want to stop.
ever.
(i know it will kill me. i dont care.)
another pottle disappears
fill me
fill me
i cant stop....
my eyes fly open like window shutters
i am shaking violently
and i am high
panic.
what have i done?
(and i have done nothing)
fire
starts my cigarette smoking
i never want to sleep again
unless it is forever.

WHY, OH GOD

DID YOU LET HIM TOUCH ME

OH GOD, WHY

HAS THE WORLD

COME CRASHING DOWN ON MY HEAD

MY INSIDES

ARE A MILLION MICROSCOPIC PIECES

THAT CANT BE PUT BACK TOGETHER AGAIN

DID I FALL OFF THE WALL

OR DID SOMEONE PUSH ME

WHY, OH GOD

ARE YOU SILENT WHEN IM SCREAMING

DISTANT

WHEN IM REACHING

OH   MY HEART!

TAKEN. MUTILATED. MAIMED.

(DESTROYED? AM I DESTROYED?)

ITS SO DARK IN HERE

SO HEAVY

AND COLD

AND I CANT FIND
ANYTHING to help me
BUT I HAVE FOUND EVERYTHING
to destroy me
WHY IS IT SO EASY
TO DEVASTATE
TO RUIN
ALL I'VE BUILT
Reconstruct me please
TAKE THIS WEIGHT AWAY
(oh, its crushing me)
DOCTOR,
I think this is serious.
WONT SOMEONE FIX ME PLEASE?
but I'll fight
WILL SOMEONE FIGHT BACK?
Somebody love me please
Please, will anybody want me?
I wish I was treasure
I wish I was NEW

I wish I could dance
Someone stole my dancing shoes
twirling, in white
like no one ever touched me
as if I wasnt ruined
As If I NEVER HAD A PRICE
dance away little girl
they are coming,
BUT IM SO GOOD AT RUNNING
(Hide away, Hide away)
WHY THE FUCK, OH GOD,
DOES IT HURT SO BAD?!
it hurts so bad that I cant feel
OH.
GOD.

I WANT TO BE A BUTTERFLY.

HOPE

Sometimes we forget
to look up.

I want to have hope
but I'm scared
I'm not familiar
with peace
I'm holding on
and I don't know
how to let go
....yet.

Today I felt my heart smile   9/12/05
deep, onto my face
a purposeful breeze
hushed over my arms
teased my hair
sighed warmly
against the nape of my neck.
A parrot
green and bursting with life
seemed to sparkle in my eyes
the violin sent comfortable chills
down my body
exhale.
My clove crackling
reassuring, between my fingers
I kick my legs over the wall
content to watch them
swing like pendulums across my perch
the sun
waves goodnight

weaving radiant streaks
of fiery purples
pinks and orange
sunkist and bloody
reds and hopeful blue
"Until tomorrow"
we whisper, soft
we never say goodbye.

9/22/05

father,
How do I forgive them?
How do I forgive
their trespasses
(no) trespassing
I should have had a sign
or would that warrant it?
I do everything I'm not supposed to
Was I just
a rule
to be broken?
They are immigrants.
Parasites.
Leeches,
sucking at my soul
forgive?
Oh father,
tell me how
how do I let go.

when they wont let go of me
(my mind).
They are photographs
forever in my head
They are everything
everywhere
I go
"father forgive them"
you said
Oh but they knew!
They knew what they were doing!,
(cries the wounded inside of me).....
forgive my unforgiving heart
and brake my legs,
so I may dance.

THEY ARE A RED TRUCK

Sebastian.

They are a guest room

They are eyes that stare
hands that touch
Bacardi 151 and Smirnoff
They are BARS
and locked car doors
AND LIES.
They are in the back seat
THEY ARE A BEST FRIEND
A HERO
Savior from church
They are a moment of isolation
couches.
Under tables or in a movie
THEY ARE everywhere I am.

I WANT TO
HOLD IT FOR YOU
—GOD

12 STEP SUMMARY

9/29/05

★ **Trust God** (process of unlocking our doors)
We have learned to lock up because
people enter w/o knocking... **GOD KNOCKS**

★ **Clean House** (responsibility) - <u>Luke 11:24-26</u>
Satan wants to attack & destroy us,
grace isn't a pill, its a move forward
that requires maintenance, we can't
allow pretty Satan to decieve us

★ **Serving Others** <u>2 Cor. 1:3-4.</u>
He comforts us in all our trouble that
we might reach out and help others.
In order to love others as we are loved
we must first experience it ourselves.
Help others: by example, with patience
and love, and gentleness.

★ <u>Micah 6:8</u> - ACT JUSTLY, WALK HUMBLY AND
LOVE MERCY ..... one day at a time

I SEE YOU.   9/30/05
and you cant have me
I FEEL YOU
cold shivers down my spine
shaking in my clammy skin
I KNOW YOU
lurking behind my back
that familiar uneasiness
tightening my throat
YOU HAVE NO PLACE HERE
stirring dischord
resentment and fear
isolating with your lies
blinding them that they may not fight
YOU LOOK SO PRETTY
lying, promisingly
in the kitchen drawer
whispering in my ear
I HEAR YOU
feeding me poison

taunting in my head

I HATE YOU

tickling my eyes

preying on the vulnerable

YOU ARE DEFEATED

and you are powerless against my armor.

I REBUKE YOU SATAN
IN THE NAME OF JESUS
CHRIST I COMMAND YOU TO
LEAVE THIS PLACE, THERE IS
NO ROOM FOR YOU HERE FOR
WHERE THERE IS LIGHT THERE
CAN NOT BE DARKNESS. FLEE.
YOUR TIME IS COMING TO AN
END. FLEE WITH YOUR TAIL
BETWEEN YOUR LEGS BECAUSE
YOU HAVE ALREADY LOST, AND
I AM VICTORIOUS IN CHRIST.

HATRED. ANGER. RESENTMENT.   tears. SIGH. HEAVY

Oh, but I can't let them out!

THE CHILD SITS AND FLIPS IN THE CORNER

the switch.   on again. off again. and

on.   and

off.   AGAIN.   AGAIN!

AND I HATE MYSELF!! fuck you.

fuck me. fuck it.....

Today is just one of those days,

where I

                HATE

                    eVeRYTHING ?

Somebody help me (leave me alone.)

        silly girl, dont you know? No one can help you.

GET THE FUCK OUT OF MY WAY

im falling im falling im falling im

        falling

and its not pretty   i wish you didn't see

me like this.

        BUT....

Masks are all so very breakable, and iu so very
destructive sir I believe id do best, to simply be.
AS UGLY AS IT MAY SEEM . and
whats the use in pretending it you cant pretend
forever? OH BUT ILL PRETEND but
I wont. I will. or will i? Oh fuck
here comes the little kid....

AND ONE LITTLE GOAT PASSES BY
FUCK UP. FUCK UP. FUCK UP. FUCK UP
FUCK UP FUCK UP. FUCK UP FUCK UP FUCK
UP FUCK UP FUCKED UP FUCK UP FUCK.
goddam that little goat.
BUT it was just a little thing
BUTS ARE SO UGLY
are they not? yet, are they not useful?
GOD FORBID THEY BE NECESARY at times.
oh hell, lets cut to the chase -
u down and out they say

IM FINE is that a lie?

IM FINE.

(fucked up, insecure, neurotic & emotional)

I WANT tO SPILL MY GUtS

without someone trying to clean them up

~~LEt THEM BE BROKEN~~ isn't it pretty?

Its pretty when they beake

when they shatter and collide

when they treuble shake and spill

WHAt a WRECK! "clean up your mess,"

he says, and disgusted, shakes his head

~~SPLIT~~ and tHE CRACKS

and I, I am useless   I am poor

"I have been weighed, I have been measured, and

I have been found WANTING"   no.... yearning

YEARNING FOR SomEtHING MORE

but I would SABATAGE myself

Yes, I take EVERYTHING away from me

I DONT DESERVE IT

There goes that negative thinking (check)
What other liabilities have I? Oh for
fucksake check them all im a goddam disgrace
   A Crying Shame

              oh, how sad is she?

Pity pity pity pity DONT YOU PITY ME
       I DID THIS TO MYSELF or did i?
I DID, I DID, ITS ALL MY FAULT
Oh, (give me give me, give me power & control)!

           A DILEMMA:

   to Sit and sulk softly, lonely in the
          DARKNESS   OR

   To RUN FAST AND FLEETING LIKE SHADOWS
   NEVER TO BE CAUGHT NEVER TO BE STILL
      But to forever be INTANGIBLE

              torn.

between   Many
           UNPLEASANT
ON AND THE CHAOS!!! paths

WHERE AM I WHO AM I and WHERE SHALL I GO?

"away, away!" pleads the voice in my head
♪ ♪ "when I wanna stay, when I wanna stay" ♪ ♪
(BRIGHT EYES.... EYES.... BETRAYERS OF MY SOUL)
and I am d
r
a
w
n

to dark greys and heavy black
red and sobbing blue

HIDE ME   express me   ME
tight and soothing comforting Please,
     make me disappear
and the bottle makes a promise of escape

ANOTHER GOAT APPROACHES THE ROADBLOCK
and I wonder, could I let him pass?

WHAT SHAME! WHAT SHAME! OH. ONLY
SHAME, SHAME AND DISGRACE HE WOULD BRING!

and could I live with that....

could I live?

WBC MEETING NOTES: 11/1/05

* This disease isn't just about drugs, its about attitudes, personalities, and behaviors.

                    ~~PRAY~~

* I have a choice about Everything. who I let in my life, what I let hurt me, etc...

* <u>Sponsor</u>- share whats really going on, get answers and apply them.

* We must constantly re-evaluate our feelings because our motives can change.

* We cant always relate in day today situations but we are always equal in the Rooms.

* We must accept ourselves fully before we stop seeking approval from others.

11/2/05

So desperate so useless and lonely, oh so lonely
dark and bitter
sad and bloody
alone in my bed, my cocoon   world away
(my) shelter shadow protection
fear you, fear me, from everything
            if only it were so
.... but how then shall I grow?
am I to let it tear me down
(the world)
being me to my knees?
and what would become of me
and could I stop the bleeding?
but for now I'll stay inside myself
with the windows closed
and the door locked tight, buried in
the covered cage of night
and shut my eyes
cradle my pain
in my arms, hooked on barbed wire

in my head
playing slideshows
for your entertainment
I've lost the remote control
I've lost
all
control
yet some small voice
begs to differ
a sliver
A hope A light of something preserved
from the decay

*HOME

I am an empty hole
I am an empty hole
am I done?
"do you want this?"
NO....   yes...   ?
funny trails
and   CIRCULAR PROBLEMS
AND.   NO SOLUTION
HELP ME (LEAVE ME ALONE)
.... let me go.
Let me break myself again
and close your eyes please   I
dont want you to see
the question is
what do we do with these
where do I go?
fill me, fill me but
you cant
I am an empty hole
I am an empty hole....

"Does he use?"   11/27/05

viciously I shake my head

(i think im trying to convince myself)

a simple omission

and some earplugs .....if only they sold earplugs for the

$$3+1\frac{1}{2}=4\frac{1}{8}|5\frac{7}{8}$$

is pounding, louder faster ANGRIER!

mind   is racing, tormenting it hates me.

SILENCE   HAS ITS PRICE

                    one...

                    TWOne.... and   THREEwo

and.... suddenly my palms are open

greedy, desperate, too many, too little

well fuck who wants to be a burden?

"YOU'RE KILLING US"

(and I wish I was only killing me)

im so confused

was this a mistake?   AND   where do I go?

AND my thoughts are rabbits, no, they are

MICE multiplying at the blink of an eye

they turn on each other,
DEVOUR THEMSELVES
until there isn't a single thought left
Oh! I dont want to think anymore .....
Its a shame I wasn't a ROBOT
(ATLEAST ID DO WHAT I WAS SUPPOSED TO.)
"YOU'LL KNOW WHEN YOU'RE DONE."
           .... I dont know ....
I DONT KNOW I DONT KNOW I DONT KNOW I DONT
KNOW I DONT KNOW I DONT KNOW I DONT KNOW.
I am done. I AM done. i am NOT done
          i am DONE.
(or should that have ended with a
question mark? perhaps no closure
at all?)
         WHAT A TERR'BLE MESS!
.. but, I cleaned up room, dont you see?
cant you be happy I did something good?
              its never good enough.
I dont compare to her   I dont compare to him.

and a fucking pencil is how i talk
  (Oh, but i talk in other ways)
  i talk with a blade against my skin
and eyes that are painted black
lips that bleed red
or a big fat smile on my face
perhaps i disapear
  but its so silent that no one hears
WHO DO YOU TALK TO WHEN EVERYONES DEAD?
Tell me, do you whisper at their graves
in hopes they'll somehow hear your cry?
    DO YOU SCREAM INTO THE ABSENCE
  THE EMPTY SPACE THAT THEY ONCE FILLED?
How do you move on
with their rotting corpses in your house?
 perhaps im a bit slow, forgive me, i am weak
I AM WEAKENED BY THEIR PRESENCE?!
I AM WEAKENED WHEN I RUN!! and....
you ask me why i pause

I think you took my breath
and I need a cigarette
and the room feels like a hospital
with muted walls that scream so loud
    where youre always alone
                        in the end
And the phone needs excuses
and it weighs a thousand pounds
and will anyone be on the other end?
    WHAT IF MY MOUTH WONT OPEN   OR
MY HEART'S TOO COLD AND THE WORDS GET FROZEN
STEADFAST IN MY THROAT AND REFUSE TO FALL
.... They are darts....
will they sting your ear when they sail
through the air and plant themselves
inside your unsuspecting head?
    too many questions   too many thoughts
too many doors and not enough locks.

11/28/05

To be beaten

<u>HELPLESS</u>

ALONE oh my god, oh god!

she left me!! panic. TRAUMA.
shock. three. they traveled in three. and
ski masks. and. we were. running.

SHE LEFT ME!! oh god, oh GOD!!
abandonment. I dont trust anyone!!
Flashing lights and questions
(I just scream) DONT TOUCH ME!!!!
I can see them beating me in the face,
slamming my skull into the car. kicking
and punching me in the head and my
neck and my ribs. oh god, oh my god!!
OH GOD, I scream. I cant stop.
NUMB. ...yet aching everywhere.
IM SCARED. IM FUCKING SCARED.
what if they come back?!!.
I crawl to my driveway. HIDE. the truck
WHY? WHY? WHY? WHY? why me?!

and im scared   like a child in the dark

they are taking me back to that place

one step away from the waiting

I HATE YOU IN YOUR STUPID UNIFORMS

I.   CANT.   SEE.   oh god....

and i dont care about the rules right now I

dont care   just get me away

blindfolds and neckbraces and pills

AND FEAR

Clingy and DETACHED

Confused and   lost

I dont know where to go

what to do or how to move (on)

EVERYTHING IS A CIRCULAR

PROBLEM

and I am an ant under a magnifying glass

I was finally half full

then someone knocked me over   and now

I am SHATTERING.

scattered thoughts
and long waves and snotting noses and
black holes
and talks you never thought you'd have
smoke filled closets
and a secret tent filled with dirt and
running as hard as you can
hands reaching
and they are there to fill their pockets and
scorn when you have nothing left
eyes, eyes
that will not look for fear of seeing themselves and
would rather die... than shed a tear
spontaneous car rides
and windows down feeling free and
very empty
screaming hard
and laughing harder we try to forget and
eventually there's gas to buy
bills to pay

and nothing ever adds up in the end and
the worlds ashamed
we have no place to go and no where to call home and
we are alone
and we quickly becomes I and
the fairytale has died
and empty bottles never quench your thirst
I am always thirsty for more
and one last cigarette, wanting to make it last
it is devoured
and instant gratification is victorious again
destroyer, destroyer
and the addict is always crying and
he never has enough
and his friends are trying to help and
hes too blind
to help himself
I wonder where the answers are
in those brief moments of clarity and
how the hell i've fallen this far

I think I want to breake away from this.
if only thinking was enough
if wanting and doing were equals and
thinking became knowing
then I'd let myself out of my cave and
embrace a sunny sky
and I would not shudder at
a smiling face
I would take my paintbrush and
tell you beautiful stories
and when you came to call on me
Id have nothing to hide
but I am far from this and I,
I am licking table tops
sucking bottles dry and
desperate enough to barter myself
to get that evasive high
someone help me please
I've got to save myself from me
I am my own worst enemy.

Another turn   2/26/06
another fork in the road
and did I choose this path
or was I pushed
the questions the questions ...
I dont want to think about tomorrow
I cant even think about yesterday
today is gone
when I close my eyes
today will last forever
I dont want the future
(remind myself to breathe)
I hate the past
where does that leave for me to go?
blink.
She's holding me
as I scream
on the couch
we are flooding the room.
blink.

He is walking away
and I scream
and I bleed
as he vanishes behind the door.
blink.
They see begging
cornering ve and I scream
I need support
Im so overwhelmed.
blink.
a new carving
fuck up, it screams
angry red
into the sink.
hate life.
this isnt how it's supposed to be
but he
he has come to take me away
I dont want to go!"
I have to I need to..... FUCK....

they want to take everything
when I have given so much
I am defiant
I am 'fiesty' (fuck yeah I am)
dont tell me, I will like it
dont tell me its ok
and I dont feel safe
I just want to escape
(and that has always been the problem)
WHAT THE FUCK DO I DO?!
the answers never surface
Im left to wander
cramped in eeriness
watched by hawks
kidnapped
held hostage
(yet, its not against my will...?!)
tomorrow is clawing at the window
its only noon
and I still dont know what the fuck to do.

LISA MERLIN HOUSE

Fuck up! (never rang so true)   2/28/06

they are always yelling at me

and I dont know what I've done

and im a cat

they are playing with me

dangling hope on a string

(please dont take it from me!!

dont take my support!!)

my friends

my family

out of for days

                                   but....

i know....   IM NOT

              ALONE.

and im talking to him and im not making sense

spasmatic thoughts

shifting eyes

the dizaness and   the shakes

sunlight dances BEHIND THE FENCE

oh how its always out of touch...

I want to hold it in my hand
yet my palms are clenching shadows
ripped off of my eyes
I poured them out onto metal & concrete
as they sat shaking their heads
  how inappropriate!"
but may I dance?   please,
I want to dance, I want to sing
and all that emerges is
stifled sobs and broken shards of heart
I suppose im somewhere in between
in the rest before the breakdown
or could I be an unexpected melody
to calm the sea after the storm
of smashing guitars and torrential screams?
and this could be my rainbow
if I stay long enough to find it
perhaps the pot of gold
will not be caged forever in my dreams
but still I sit and sulk in rain clouds

afraid of falling down
I just need someone to push me
someone to show me how
and here I am
dazed and confused
my head is foggy and I cant see
past the darkness of now
clinging to my suitcase
wanting to find home
hoping someone will see me
and ease my way as I let go.

Im waking up on pins & needles   3/1/06
with a head full of glass
I try to smile
today is new and bright and
cold
It greets my nose with its frigid breath
and harsh beams of prodding light
stabbing through my eyes
I want desperately to recoil
to burry myself deep into my covers,
Oh! cover me, cover me cover me....
and I miss my friends and I dont want to think
about them
they are dead
in this new life
their tombstones litter my heart
I try to smile
and late night talks
I share my hope, my answer I
tell her about the empty hole

and the only thing that can fill it
without flowery words
or religous babble (babble, babylon....)
no liquid no powder no pills down my throa
can stand in the gap.
no child no man no matter
how much fat you suck off your stomache
we have an empty hole
an empty hole
Fill me!! Fill me!! we cry
WE SCREAM
with fistfulls of answers
we self medicate   and shattered
turn our faces to the sky in silent protest
Why? why.
If only they could realize
the answer was just that
Oh, dont forget to look up....
Focus, focus on yourself they say, focus on 'me'
but im on pins & needles
and im dying to bleed.

but today is new and i
ive left my razor blades
behind
i grab a pencil and some dead trees
and scratch my heartache
into them instead
it lacks the power
of red
and it feels too soft,
too shy and
unsure
when you try to scream with lead
i try to smile,,
....but i dont want to try,
i want my heart to flutter and expand
until my lips begin to tickle
and run, bursting to my ears
unable to stop them
to deter their flight
ill stand there helpless, hopeful

and wave goodbye to tears
but for now I am
face down
stuck inside the mud
all I want
is a helping hand
someone to pull me up
and I'll seize every moment here
fight with all I am
this isnt the life Im meant to lead
there's so much more
so much more
if I only choose to take it
if only I believe.

*Positive thought: 3/1/06
  • I started on my step work by
myself, & completed up to #28 so far
  • I haven't been yelled at and I'm
on time getting up, good day!!
FUCK THIS SHIT.   3/1/06
I FUCKING WANT TO GO HOME
HATE LIFE HATE THEM HATE ME
I WANT MY FRIENDS YOU MUTHERFUCKERS
I fucking hate everything,
FUCK YOU AND YOU MOTHERFUCKERS

— Dan's Meeting —

*As addicts we want our recovery   3/2/06
RIGHT NOW!! However, we didn't wake up &
decide to become addicts, it was a process
just like this program.

* recovery is a process of peeling away
1 layer at a time, our body/mind can't
handle it all at once (💡 thats why I can
only cry/feel pain for so long before I
shut off)

Today I'm grateful for: 3/3/06
1- A big sister   2- The groceries we got!
3- The relationships I'm developing 4- meetings
5- Laughter

I'm grateful for: 3/4/06
1- Christina 2- having some 'me time'
3- Going out to a meeting 4- a shower
5- getting to Relax & friendship w/ the girls

MY GOALS — (by weeks)

1. Get a sponsor ✓   2. Call Sponsor,
3. Work Steps   4. Stay clean & sober)

Im Thankful For: 3/5/06
1. Im thankful to see everyone enjoying
their families
2. Im thankful for a good meeting w/
my case manager
3. Im thankful for a pertinent issue
being discussed It our in house meeting
4. Im thankful we get to watch a
movie
5. Im thankful for the ability to
laugh It myself

IM THANKFUL FOR: 3/6/05
1. The ODAT meeting   2. Finishing Step One   .
3. A great lunch   4. Good meeting w/ Judy
5. Rediscovering the Joy in SKIPPING!!

(SPEAKER AT SMO? SAT. NIGHT)
... LAS VEGAS...
(417) 926 - 3883
Christina @

"I CANT STOP DRINKING" she cries   3/6/05
my heart breaks
skin crawls
there's so much more to life than this.
there's so much more
than lying face first in the mud
drowning in our addiction
swallowing lungfulls of hopelessness
there is so much more
than the fishooks of despair
yanking at our insides
than the darkness and the rain
there is reaching
and wings and flying
there are shoulders
to carry us when we are too weak
I want to scream about hope
and life and love
a love big enough to hug a muddy addict
and I want to scream

because the weight of her tears
is sinking me in this room
I feel the water rising
my head bobs above the surface....
but I just sit and weep
and light another cigarette
Oh, there's got to be so much more
than *this* !!
Its moments like these that I feel like a child
and I dont understand and I want to know
WHY and I want 'mommy' to come floating
down out of the sky and explain and justify
this life and hold me with the salt in my eyes...
But it's not okay,
I hate this *fucking* disease
I have always been attracted to Destruction
(destroy me, destroy me please)
darkness was my blanky
and chaos ran with me
but today I hate you

you are my enemies
I hate watching you dismember
cripple.
Maim.
and   and.
today I wish I were a lighthouse
to keep you from peril
I wish I were a beam of sunshine
dancing in your hair
I want to show you Happiness
and help you kill Despair.
But I just sit and weep and smoke
and tug your shaky hand
I mutter a few words
choke on a catch phrase or two
you hug me and tell me I'm pretty
and pat me on the back
I walk out feeling like that silly brat
that always got a cookie
and all I wanted was to tell you that....
(There's so much more than this.)

~ ODAT ~   3/7/06

* The Number One killers of addicts are:

    1. ANGER   2. RESENTMENT

"Resentment is the poison we make for
someone else, but kills US.
(what resentments am I hanging onto?)

I'M THANKFUL FOR: 3/7/06

1. A delicious dinner   2. A shower 3. My hair 'cooperating'

4. The ODAT meeting 5. Sharing in Steve's group

I'm thankful for: 3/8/06

1. the ODAT meetings 2. food to eat 3. a lazy day

4. Readings 5. getting up on time

I'm thankful for: 3/9/06

1. Christina's friendship 2. Talking to Judy

3. The ability to be real 4. I wasn't the one who left

5. My big sister & the kitties 6. Rebecca's story

I'm thankful for: 3/10/06
1. My Sponsor 2. A new Meeting 3. New contacts

4. Cigarettes 5. On time to medication

1. Laying out 2. In-House meeting 3. letting go   3/11/
4. The lessons I'm learning 5. Christina's back safe

SOMETIMES I THINK MY WHOLE LIFE IS A LIE   3/7/06

AND I WONDER IF I EVEN KNOW THE TRUTH

I FEEL SO SMALL

AND MY PROBLEMS ARE SO

BIG

IM DIGGING CUTS (INTO MY NAILPOLISH)

LOATHING THE GRATING MAN ON THE TELEVISION

I WANT TO PUNCH HIM IN THE FACE

DONT YOU WALK AWAY FROM ME!

and tears roll down my angry cheeks

sleep tugs at my brain

beckons, seduces

she tempts me with her numbness

she wants to be my new cocaine

AND I SUCCUMB AND I FEEL SO SMALL

I want to disappear

but I cant I wont

that's not why Im here

and so I open my mouth (heart)

attempt to identify

the specimens of rock
and glass or blood inside
I try to disect
the massive ball of fury
before the switch flips off
and I cant see
but my eyes are glazing over
staring, becoming empty space
im not ready to fight yet
my muscles are too weak
but, today I began to feel the weight,
to take a step,
toward a victory so sweet.

..... AND THEN TAMMY LEFT....,

i feel sad and angry so   3/9/06

and oh so huet

and shocked that i feel at all, and

i dont know what's worse....

they speak of bieng calloused,

(when iu learning to be soft)

they saye better her .

than ue

this is a selfish program

(but my heart! my heart!)

it beats, it bleeds

in turmoil, in restlessness

and it begs my feet

to chase her down,

there is no garuntee

too many have walked away

have crawled helplessly, blindly

into early graves

my eyes give birth to tiny rivers

the boa in my throat constructs

my head is spinning, shaking
body rocks and quivers
I begin to loose control
Oh!!! I am powerless!!
But I have the power of prayer
She gets on Her knees,
cups Her palms
as if holding her there
and offers them up to God
(keep her, keep her)
We've got to let go
and its not easy, and its not fair
but theres no other way we know.
So I hold myself, remember to breathe,
banish my evil thoughts
find closure in the absence of her things
then move on / move on
as God whispers
"My child, sweet child,
you are growing wings."

3/10/06

Lord, help me view my recovery with the
same gravity I viewed Tammy's
yesterday. There is never any
guarantee, that is why I am done.
Keep me fresh, Give me eyes, to see,
ears to hear, and a heart to
understand, and help me to cont.
to let go. Thank you.

~SWOT~   3/10/06

* If you aren't willing to stop, no one can
help you, however, when you want to quit,
then it becomes my concern.

* KEEP COMING BACK.

* learn to be Grateful, we have a
choice over how we view things.

* There is NEVER an excuse to use

* Thank God life isn't fair, I am fortunate
to have alluded the consequences A my actions.

I am   3/12/06

a tooth

with the root

EXPOSED!!

In thankful for: 3/14/06

1. Getting up on time for meditation.

2. The treadmill 3. I get to see my dad today

and my family 4. I have phone privledges

5. People sharing cigarettes with me

* Our lives are tornadoes.... (in addiction) 3/14

* We create ripples with every action/decision,

it effects everyone we've touched not

just ourselves

* I AM an alcoholic - pg. 21 in The Big Book

* When I get complacent & think I can drink,

" I reverested, in slight" symptom, read pg 24

OKAY - HALF MEASURES AVAIL US NOTHING

* Instant Gratification is the ever illusive dream

we seek   Фсё, я не могу делат ишу.

* ACCEPTANCE

Central   3/13/06

* MY RECOVERY COMES FIRST
* I need to 'double chek' my words/actions
   (do I really want to do this?)
* I cant go into the teenches and pull people
out, I need to wait for theu to reach out
a hand for help. (LET GO.)
* Many will die so soue will stay....
* "...Life is heavy..." that's why we need prayer
and fellowship
* THERE IS NEVER AN EXCUSE TO USE - ask for help
* The people who want it, will get it.
* I can play with the devil or I can
enjoy God's miracles, THIS IS NOT A GAME,
if I use I face spleitual & physical death,
if I abstain I can experience a beautiful life.
- ContaCtS -

_____

_____

_____

В поцусски я говоц в Бог   3/14/06

фсё, Я не мочу делат шшу.
мне не нраветься Что Я зделат,
и Я не хочу зделат шшу,
           Слава Богу !!

Бог,

помочите позалуста, Вы я нузно.
Я не мочу делаю фсё некада все
вы. Спасибо. Я тебя люблю.

                    Рэне

≥CENTRAL≤   3/15/06

* Ask God for clarity (daily)
* Live in the solution
* Rebirth (what's my experience? How has
God saved me? In what ways do I need to
be reborn today?)
* The answer to the problem is ACCEPTANCE.
* I dont have to 'figure it out' I just need to do it.
* DONT ANALYZE, UTILIZE!!

I'm thankful for: 3/15/06

1. An amazing time with my family yesterday

2. The girls here showing they love me

3. Kristin & Farley fighting to be my big sister

4. Mallory leaving me her flowers

5. Getting my cigarettes w/ Liz & Kelly

I'm thankful for: 3/16/06

1. A good 'ANGER' group w/ Joan 2. My God Box

3. Support by my sisters here 4. The lessons I'm learning

5. Strengthened relationship w/ God

I'm thankful for: 3/17/06
1. Going to bed early last night 2. New shampoo

3. The cats 4. food to eat 5. A meeting

I'm thankful
for: 1. A treat at the meeting   3/18/06

2. Going to a meeting 3. Getting to watch a movie

4. A new roommate 5. A good hair day!

I'm thankful
for: 1. Spending the day with my family   3/19/06

2. The gifts they brought 3. Getting my eyebrows waxed

4. A great dinner 5. A good meeting with Judy

6. My dreams/purpose beginning to be fulfilled

7. A meeting 8. Movie time!!

— Mallory —

WHY DID YOU LEAVE ME!!!!   3/15/06

I feel so abandoned
defenceless, betrayed.
And dead flowers
are supposed to make it ok?!
The SHOCK of an empty bed
like a coffin
punched me in my stomache
(Flip the switch)
I am in
denial.   and then
the flood
a rush of blood to the head
I lay there shaking
holding myself
bleeding mascara on your grave
the stabbing
throbbing, salty wound
one minute I'm calm
the next I'm insane
It hits like waves

and. I ho

I HURT SO BAD.

fuck you dead plants
I want to stomp on them,
scatter them against the wall.   but.
I want to hold them
cherish them
because maybe you thought of me
before you fucked us all

I love you
I hate you
            IM SCARED.
I cant make you stay
I cant make you want it
but I know I do
and I'll do whatever it takes
I cant kill my family anymore
and I dont want to kill myself
your absence has only given me
   something else to fight for.

Winter Park Group   3/17/06

* Alcoholism is a PROGRESSIVE disease:
(Each relapse is worse, when I am tempted to
drink, remember the last time - the worst - and
know it will only digress if I pick up.)
* I can't depend on the people around me,
I only control myself, my sobriety is my
responsibility. (when people walk out, it's
not an excuse for me to use.)
* Fear is an ENEMY (a remedy: Step One)
It nags but through my God I can
defeat it.
        CONTACTS

JEN - ███████████   (red hair, irish)
Randi - ██████████

"...FAILURE IS <u>NOT</u>
FALLING DOWN,
IT'S STAYING
DOWN."

— Debbie at ORLO VISTA

* falling down is an opportunity to get up,
it is only when I refuse to learn that I
have failed.

* No one can save me from myself (if I
dont want it, I wont have it.... only through
My Higher Power, and turning my will over)

* Remember the DESPAIR, the moments
when you wanted to DIE.... Do you
Really want to go back?!

* When I was in my addiction my dreams
were merely dreams, in my RECOVERY my
dreams are being Realized.

There is Hope for something more

.... this isnt all there is.

* There is pain and suffering, and great loss
in this world, but we can find strength
and hope in the Rooms.

* EGO - edging God out

TO WRITE LOVE ON HER ARMS

(feature article of
Relevant magazine)
.... MY STORY!!....
        THANK YOU.

3/19/06

3/20/06

Thank you for teaching me so much about you. Thank you for answering my prayers. My dreams are coming true and this is only the beginning!! WOW....

There are no words to express the way it feels to see a purpose for my pain, that, is what I have *longed* for, for SO long. That is what has driven me and given me hope through all the darkness. You take my mess and turn it into something beautiful. Please continue to use me in powerful ways, make me a shining star in the Universe father, I want to SHINE for you. Thank you for all you've already done, for all you are doing, and for everything you are going to do. I love you, I love you, I love you, I love you. And please help me remember, its all about You.

THANKFULS: 3/20/06

1. Iu thankful for groceries 2. Jesha's graduation

3. special dinner 4. A beautiful day today

5. Going to the ODAT meeting.
                                              3/21/06
          BIG BOOK STUDY W/ DIANE

* When I begin to deny that I am indeed

an alcoholic, read | pg. 30 | (More about Alcoholism)

THANKFULS:
1. Iu SO thankful that Tricia is my sponsor!! 3/21/06

2. Iu SO thankful my sponsor is visiting me Sunday

3. Iu thankful for a good session w/ Steve

4. for an amazing dinner 5. for another day sober

Thankfuls:
                                              3/22/06
1. Iu thankful for YOGA today 2. Going to SWOT

3. A good talk w/ a sister 4. A new day 5. My sponsor

          ~ SWOT ~   3/22/06

* When Iu angry about people managing my

money, I need to remember its to teach me

structure, accountability, & earn trust. (what

would I do w/ it anyway?!)

* In our addiction we depended on others, that's

why NA is self-sufficient   ⟶

**★★ ITS NOT THE <u>ISSUES</u> THAT ARE IMPORTANT,
    ITS THE <u>FEELINGS</u>.**

★1 create more shit in my life than
anyone else ever could

★ Anger - love, call others,
  fear - call, talk, unrealistic fears!

  Resentment - call others, discuss it let it go

· Our mind tricks us into playing into our
disease

★ WE NEED TO WORK AS HARD CHASING OUR
RECOVERY AS WE DID OUR DRUGS.

INFORMATION + APPLICATION =
    ★ *Transformation* ★

HELP
↓↓
make the
connection.

CONTACTS: outside Jen (407) ████████
★
There's a line between having the humility to
ask for help, and being dependent on others
(GIVE BACK)

★ YOU ALWAYS NEED THE ROOMS, WE ARE
PROGRESSIVELY ILL. The symptoms may
lesson, but it is still there and treatment is needed

★ GRIEVE - Anger is a part of grief. Its OK
to be angry.

I remember that darkness   3/22/06
where my heart was caged
in turmoil, contaminated, poisoned, I
needed a place
to wait out the storm, to cleanse
somewhere safe, where
blood letting
is o.k.
No one to clean up my mess
or fix me
No threat of an ambulance
of white sterile walls
or police
I was pushed to speak
and forced to lock up
offered a place to fall & rest my head
and at the last minute
spotting the nails
lying in my bed
the fear

the peessuee, the
volcano pushing, pushing
and no one sate
to teust, to reassuee
I was gaueded
in need of a confidant
and here I found
the key
the Roous
oh please! ....please,
dont.
take that.
away from me.

"Lord, make me a channel of thy peace — that
where there is hatred, I may bring love —
... where there is wrong, I may bring the
spirit of forgiveness — where there is discord,
I may bring harmony — where there is error,
I may bring truth — ... doubt, I may bring
faith — where there is despair, I may bring
hope — ... shadows, I may bring light, that
where there is sadness I may bring joy.
... may I seek ... to comfort than be comforted —
to understand than be understood — to love
than to be loved ... It is by self-forgetting
that one finds ... by forgiving that one is
forgiven ... by dying that one awakens to
Eternal Life. Amen."

* God's worst plan for us is better than my best.
* "Thy will, not mine, be done.
   often when I pray for myself & others I think I know
what His will is, I need to ask.

WE CAN'T TRANSMIT WHAT WE DON'T HAVE

Im thankful for: 3/23/06

1. Laurer 2. A loving community 3. June's graduation

4. Talking to my Sponsor 5. Aush
                                                    3/24/06

THANKFULS:

1. Spending time w/ Austi 2. Being able to share
safely in this meeting 2. SNOI 4. Having 30
days clean 5. Getting to see my sponsor tonight

Winter Park Group   3/24/06

* Many are called, few are chosen. (?)
* When someone leaves, don't take it personal.
Learn from their mistakes, use it to help
keep me sober.
* Remember you where the one who left before
* It gets better, as long as I dont pick up.
* Be the change you seek
* Dont shut down, dont give up. there is hope
(Remember the promises) → (pg 11, into 3/14)

CONTACTS: Rebecca S. ██████████
█ Christine - ██████████ (blond hair)
                                       + tattoo
Anna - ██████████ (child)

Last night he came to me   3/24/06
again
in my sleep
came to
as opposed
to came after
and, I wanted
I longed
sickly sweet
and bitter in my heart
my mind was swimming
is swimming
fear and loathing and love?
and hate and
GUILT
he seemed so soft, inviting
he was magnetic
guilt for running away
wanting now to run to
missing his feel

kissing....

and disturbed

how disturbing to love

a thorn in my side

and your lips are haunting

your lips

followed by a fist

contusion

turmoil   and

                    chaos

and is it love?

this detrimental attachment

you haunt me

there in the darkness

behind my eyes

inside my chest

and

I never want to sleep again.

I dont even want to breath

I want you to go away
and beg you not to leave. sick. so sick. and sorry. sorry

* ~~We are not alone in the Rooms~~
* Keep your head up, good things will come
* Keep writing to expose the ROOT
* I never want to go through '30' again, remember the weight of the wave I created by running, face it now before its too big.
* God will calm the storm, or calm me.
* STAY [dont] leave before the miracle happens !!
* The difference between drugs and a blade is the method.

CONTACTS: Harriet ████████████ (chair person)
████████████ Dee (chair) / KNOW PAIN, good to talk to

30 DAYS CLEAN
3/24/06

I hate my mind   3/24/06
so sick and disturbing
I hate you
and me and everything
FUCK YOUR PINK CLOUD
lu dark and stormy
and grey
heavy. heavy.
and raining
I want to rain on your parade
lu choppy and sharp and soft
lu scratchy and textured
intricate
woven
into so many things
feel me.
I can
and.
I feel you
but your unsettling

too soft
the kind for squeezing
hard
that makes you grind your teeth
and the rage
your sunlight is blinding
and I'm still waiting for rain
like tears
falling. falling.
the soft pitter patter
a heavy sigh
the world is my insides
moody and shifting and restless
and.
appropriate.
the wave has been chasing
growing
as I ran and
now the stand still
the calm

as the ocean
gathers itself
to swallow me
crush me
TREAD.
(keep your head afloat)
thirty days
and thirty nights
praying for the end
tossing and turning
tormenting dreams
shadows and shadows
and.
            STILL...
                    the beating of wings
keep coming back
they say
im staring at my arms
stay, stay
as the cuts fade to scars

and like scars in' healing
the pain remains
It is my story that I wear
evident
burning
a stinging cleanse
scrubbing the dirty wounds inside
so that I can share.
Oh hope, o distant hope
dont hide your face from me
COME BACK!!
my arms ache from reaching
how long
Oh God, HOW LONG
am I to be beaten by the waves
deliver me from the depths
the dark creatures
playing in my memories
the sun will rise, rise and.
hope comes in the morning. (mourning).

★ LORD, PLEASE HOLD YRLCY
DORY

1. The walk 2. face painting 3. a back message

4. coffee at the park 5. Going to a meeting

6. Tracy's safety

~ SWOT ~   3/25/06

★ Be grateful for crashing, sometimes
its the first step to recovery.

★ Remember dual-diagnosis
(Many addicts have another factor
contributing to their disease)

★ God uses pain, we dont always see it
immediatley .... TRUST. (pain isnt always bad)

★ Allow yourself to grieve
★ Dont ask why .... ACCEPTANCE

THANKFULS: 1. Seeing my sister 2. Getting to know Tracy2
3/26/06
3. Watching TV 4. the Eating Meeting 5. A month clean

thankfuls:
3/27/06 1. Going to SWOT 2. Nice weather 3. Getting
to give my sister my 30 day key tag 4. A safe
place to sleep 5. Having Tracy2 for a sponsor
6. Time with Laura 7. Popeyes! 8. Tim's graduation

I am dark and heavy
and hostile.
fragile. and.
confused. I
need someone
to let me rain.
who knows
what it is to bleed
to be
abused.

Friday Night Live Contacts:

Jessica ▓ ████████████████,

(Also at SW07, knee surgery, curly hair)

~ OBAT ~   3/26/05

* The geographical 'cure':
its niave to think we can move and leave
all our problems behind.

* YET - it is _always_ yet as long as
we continue to use.

* Pain and suffering can create beauty
if we allow God to use it.

* With blessings come temptation & trials,
STAND STRONG.

* Dont compare stories, identify w/ the _feelings_.

* _If_ you want what they have, _Do_ what they do

* WHO AM I WHEN NO ONE
  IS LOOKING?

* This disease is _CUNNING, BAFFELING, AND_
  POWERFULL. We make mistakes.

* _DONT_ take on another person (relationship)
until you've taken on YOURSELF.

* SHIT still happens in sobriety, all that matters
is that I stay clean. ("...ATLEAST I AM SOBER.")

* Just because I stopped using, it doesn't mean that all my problems are going to disappear, there's a lot of work to do!! (That's why recovery is a process.)

* When I form a reservation, am I glamorizing my disease? Remember the *destruction* and the *despair*.

* Live life on life's terms

* We all earned our seats here, don't forget it.

Thankfuls: 3/28/06

1. A meeting 2. Family counseling 3. Hope in recovery
4. Lisa Merlin House 5. My recovery

SCARS ★

Tattoos with better stories....

Thankfuls:
3/29/06 1. The gift from my parents 2. Seeing a fellow cutter
3. GOAT meeting 4. Being able to laugh 5. A good book

"... Out of every season of grief or suffering, when the hand of God seemed heavy or unjust, new lessons for living were learned ... resources of courage were uncovered ... and the conviction that God does "move in mysterious ways His wonders to perform.""

* DRAW NEAR TO ME, AND I WILL DRAW NEAR TO YOU. As we improve our relationship life makes remarkable ; unexpected turns for the better. (Step 11 on a daily basis)

* Before you lash out ... pray
(Sometimes we get "He can wait" syndrome.)

* Prayers are petition, meditation: listen

Thankfuls 3/30/06 1. The gifts on my bed 2. Aush 3. My sponsor 4. Speah 5. A bottom bunk

3/31/06: 1. Sleepover!! 2. Friday Night Live 3. A chance to get out of the house 4. The Article June wrote 5. Getting the letter from Ashley

THANKFULS: 1/1/06

1. The ability to restrain my temper today

2. Visitation tomorrow 3. Going to SWOT

4. A good relationship w/ my sponsor 5. Austi

OWN CONTACTS

TAMI █████████████ ("nice eyes, gum)
                              (van eiderrr!)

* Pray for Christine ^{shes} (2 weeks) all the good I
want for myself

Thankfuls
     1/2/06: 1. A good visit with my parents 2. Finishing
Step One w/ Tricia 3. Establishing a relationship w/ Christine
from WPG 4. A phone card 5. Shes apologizing... "

4/3/06
1. GETTING PHASED UP 2. A good talk w/ my sponsor

3. A bottom bunk 4. Food 5. Prayer

4/4/06 1. LMH 2. Judy 3. In house meetings

4. God testing me 5. Sarah's friendship

4/5/06 1. Going to ODAT 2. Meeting Christine there

3. Listening to music 4. No makeup 5. The Promises

4/6/06 1. Judy's Concoction 2. Finishing another book

3. Finding my jacket!! 4. A good book to read

5. I get to go to FNL in a CAR Friday!

that there's a lot of money I'm going to be in
debt with, LMH, phone bill, college is on me, $\frac{1}{3}$
whatever else... BLAH!! But I know it'll be taken
care of as long as I do 'the next right thing'...
GOOD FOR YOU! I'M SO PROUD OF YOU FOR
REALIZING WHAT'S REALLY UP! WAY TO GO MY LITTLE
ONE! Thank you my love! Baby's
growing up! Ha, next step, potty training.

OKAY   1/4/06

* ACCEPTANCE is the answer to all my problems
* If I am disturbed with something, there is a
problem w/ me
* NOTHING HAPPENS BY MISTAKE
* Dont concentrate on how the world needs to
change, concentrate on what needs changing in me.
* unless I accept life on life's terms I can
not be happy.
* LIVE IN THE SOLUTION not the problem.
* "If your on a journey for revenge, make
sure you dig TWO graves." — OKAY

CHRYSALLIS

Dark and bitter   4/8/06
and cold, so cold
I beat myself, everyday
I bleed to teach you
lessons I never learned
FUCK UP! FUCK UP!
the razor screams
He grabs her arms
He's on his knees
trying to show her a softer way
white dresses, white dresses
and starlit skies
dancing, twirling
from the inside
...! this is how its meant to be
and it feels so good to be clean
Oh! keep your poison
I've had enough
and they have written love
over the pretty pink scars

* THIS IS ME. *   3/1/05

This is me

It is dark and yes, its black (☺)

It is different from what you are

and it spins.

It is different from what you are

and its mine.

Was not my hand that took

up these weights

to tie them on my back.

Was not my head that woke

up Sad, and

placed Happy on a hanger.

But it is my *heart*

that writes these words

have been engraved upon it

and I sit here as a simple phrase

levitates above the rest:

THIS IS ME.

I like the repetition.

I like that line and this whole thing reminds me of you, but of course! THIS IS you!

EISLEY ☆ @ HOB

w/ REGGIE & THE FULL EFFECT
ELUCIDATION

AND
New found Glory (BAD NASTY!!)

SMOKING porch

"Y-O-U-E..." "loooue"

ME & Osbourne
(and Lexi)

Dillan & Kaysi

↓ Circus!!

A Mockery of Emo girl pics

"There's sharks in there!!"

THE JUDGING LINE

"...NFG... NFG... Eisley?... NFG... They're lost... NFG..."

$1,000,000,000 \times 10^{999}$ NFG shirts

Hotwheels
Fire engine

pizza turnables

just Phob

Right foot, left foot
one infront of the other,
glance down
the cracks.

THE CRACKS....

1, 2, 3, 4, 5,.... 6   six
perfect gaping cracks
in the sidewalk
I glance down
(twelve minutes ago)

Right to left
grip the handle, one after the other
a knock on the door
somebody help me please

You hurt everyone
and he is choking on salt
You hurt everyone
and I am going buy salt

My blood is your blood
spilling out upon the carpet
spilling out onto the trash can
spilling (how clumsy of we)
from the cracks

And the ghosts
dance out from my open mouth
like a smoggy genie shrouded in grey
dance away, blue grey
(in the humming spotlight of the streetlight)

A thin layer of soot
covers the ground infront of we
I dont even look up tonight
Im studying the cracks.

And back home I know he is choking on salt.

I LIKE:

* finding the cold spot on my pillow
* Chenelle blankets
* Dark greys
* Stretching
* Eating Cheez-Its when I'm sad
* Snuggling
* Coffee & cigarettes
* The perfect texture of my bed in the morning
* Skirts that twirl
* People on my right side
* Linking arms
* Tight hugs
* Doing things just because I can
* Even numbers
* Butter on my pop tarts
* Telling Grant I'm full so I can give him my food
* Riding in the car
* Sleeping with no socks on
† Eye flirting

I DON'T LIKE:

* The sound of people chewing their food
* Tying my shoelaces
* When people annunciate every letter
* Happy people in the mornings
* Cafeterias
* The smell of old people
* Apple skins
* Tags in my shirt
* Booming voices
* Holding hands
* Light touch
* Chapped lips
* Colored contacts
* Rap/R&B/hiphop
* The left side/odd numbers
* Sleeping w/o music
* Being over analyzed
* Jelly
* Washing my jeans or sweatshirts
* People trying to make you talk
* Turtle necks

3/18/05

Underneath the stars
Underneath the blankets
blending together
in a melody
carried by guitar strings
carried by the calm
of the lake
as she faithfully held
the sky in her belly
snuggling into spaces
too small to contain us
to contain our shivering bodies
We fly away
to higher ground
to pillowy make shift beds
to fall to the floor
and he is breathing in my ear
breathing on my ear
and on my neck
soft   and it tingles
soft   and I'm pretty

melting in his arms
but I'm fighting
resisting — giving in
My lips brush his
lips
hover
and land gentle
and the sounds
begin to dewind
unordered by the beating
of our hearts
toss and turn
playful, tearing
and the hands
run
in passionate circles
I can hear the past
chasing them in a fury
and flashing lights
hide the lies
hide the laughter in our voices
to hide.

to run away from what it is
to hold True in our hands
and shake it
like fireflies in a jar
and catch it
before it falls
clattering
in pieces
on the floor
we squeeze it into the center
of our palms
and decide when to let it go
or suffocate it in our grasp
and the hands
run
in passionate parallels
i can hear the past
screaming as they draw close
screaming
but not tonight
tonight he holds my lips instead
"you're too special for that"

and the joy
and pain
and sorrow and remorse
regret and relief
cultivate
collect
in my eyes
and drop like dew
from the petals of a rose
drop
like a penny
from a careless pocket
heads or tails
it matters not
all that is significant
is that it fell
and they fell, oh they fell
to kiss his shoulder
and drove me home
to gather myself
into sheets
and collapse into my pillow.

* 3/22/05 @ THE SOCIAL *

COPELAND

CD RELEASE PARTY

w/

LOVEDRUG

ACCEPTANCE

Steph Alice

My brother & Beared
:(wouldn't go

Ryan

♪ Le tigre dance parties ♪
♪ in the car ♪

autographs on
my ticket and cd
jacket sleeve

PICTURES W/ Lovedrug
and Aaron Marsh

DEBUT OF THE
RED LIPSTICK

Wocka
Frapaccinos

A watered hott
singer hott gorgous
watered duck "

I sit here in the night   4/4/05
writing in the golden glow
of the streetlight
writing in the glow
of the moonlight
all alone,
its just me and the writing on the wall
they watch me cry
I break & fall
they watch me shake
and say nothing at all
I cant say anything
at
all.
The words are pounding inside my head
to be let out
someone sealed my mouth w/ cement
and they are suffocating
me
I cant breath
I   cant   breath
get out.

The room grows dark
and cold
and i am the only one on my side
a whirely top
circus ride
nothing's making sense
and i am lost
dont touch me
so soft
it ont right
dont speak
so kind
it hurts me
and i cant breath
yu not running away
please dont teaue the questions
oh they're the wrong questions
and you are lawyers
and they say
jump in the lake and drownd
jump in the lake and drownd
jump in the lake and drownd

but I wont
they cant have us
bash your head
into the bridge
they say
(they whisper)
oh' They scream
but I will silence them
you bastards
and it is cold
and I cant go back
I cant go back
I CANT GO
BACK.
and I am breaking their hearts
and I am destroying them
destroying us
us.
Im so helpless
there are no answers
only the cracks in my skin
they are marred now

And they are watching me bleed
frantic.
helpless.
nurture.
bandage.
And they are washing my blood
off the bridge
scrubbing it off with their faces
watching me bleed
they make streams
run from their eyes
and my tears are crying into the sink
onto his shirt
all over the bridge
they collect my shameful tears
and bury them in white cloth
and I hate the stars tonight
I envy their perfection
envy their calm
silent watch over me
one day I'll join
one day I'll find peace

but until then they will serve for me
and i will watch them
silently
i will watch them
and wonder
what it is like
to shine through black
airless night
and touch so many
touch so many
and i will love them
take their hope
swallow them whole
they'll shine through my eyes
and scatter the shadows
in that house.

MICHELLE

And she is crying   4/6/05
calling
out to me
trying to reach me through
the telephone lines
and I am here
sweet child
I am here
and I am listening
I always have been
listening
to your bruises
with my stethescope ears
to your arms
with my first aid kit
heart
for you
And she is crying
calling
out (to God?)
where is love
it comes balled up

in clenched fists
flying
harsh against her skin (heart)
and she is falling
hard on the tile floor
it recieves her
more than her father ever has
and I am here
sweet child
I am here
and I am listening
I always will be
listening
to your bruises
with my stethescope ears
to your arms
with my first aid kit
heart
for you
and I love you
with my arms
wrapped tight around your shoulders

shaking
and I love you
with words
that kiss your ears
with fingers
running gently
through your hair
and I'll miss you
with my eyes
but I know
sweet child
that the sun
will keep on rising
that the stars
will keep on shining
and I will always love you
I will always be here
and I'm listening
with my heart
for you.

Homeless

It is gone.

my safe haven
my world away

has been torn apart
dismantled.
removed.
erased.

They have dismembered it
painted soft
soothing pastel
grass
over my blood
my tears

my memories

they have painted a period
permanently at the end of the sentence.

and I have forever lost it
my home
and I am no one
I am no where
I have nothing
.... and so much more than that

and it stings.

the absence
resides heavily
in my eyes
creeps
slyly
down my cheeks.

do they miss me?
(the walls)
that once held
me
my story
my pain ?

The red
blue
lies burried underneath
waiting for me
so they may breath

but it is forbidden
they will suffocate
in that airless coffin
made for someone else

they are supposed to hold ME.

It is threashing around inside
mildly
but i will drown it
I will tip one back
to fight the haunting
the misery

of being homeless.

it has been taken from me
No, i did not give so freely
as you might think,
i did not look as readily
at her
and she should have been crying
into the bathroom sink
but her eyes where too dry
too numb
to feel the loss
to mourn the death
of her dream
it passed away
with her eyes closed
gripping the door
in the black night
it has been shattered
and lies hollow
on the concrete
rotted, forlorn
and so dissapointed

and so forsaken
and she is lamenting
hushed, bottled, poison
inside herself
subconsciously wandering
back to the scene
of the crime
pictures flash
a slideshow
oh! what a terrible movie
I never wanted to see
but somehow it keeps playing
and I can't make it stop
please won't someone make it cease
it is haunting me
and I am robbed of everything
I had locked secure
inside my heart
and he is victorious
and I am lame
I am lost
the piano

mourns for me
a beautiful song
melancoly
dripping, falling
weary
from the weight
of the hands that play
and they arent mine
I am lulled to sleep
by the silence
of falling stars
and i too am falling
plummeting
from my nest
in the clouds
he has clipped my wings
and i cant fly
he has choked me
torn out my vocal chords
and i cant sing
what use is a nightingale
without a song?

what good is a guitar
that has no strings?
what use is a promise
that has been broken?
what is the purpose
of a ring that I can't wear?
my heart is broken
into a million microscopic pieces
miserable and weak
longing to be whole
as it lies fragmented
at my feet
but i can't control them
long enough to make them stop
and pick up the remainders
so i am useless
used
heartsick and hopeless
wallowing in the anguish
of my defeat.

4/12/05

The outline of the palm tree
a scarecrow strapped to his post
begging, pleading to be set free
and he is me
and me are one
tossed in the wind
tangled, trapped, inside myself
but all I want is to let go
but I am holding me so close
I just want to escape
won't someone help me please
help me stop, get away
this liquid, it intoxicates
and I'm afraid
I am bitter, I am angry
I'm pathetic, oh so sad
oh so lonely
so far
too close
for comfort
save me for God's sake....

the past holds me tight
secure.
familiar.
I dont know what else is out there
outside the shadows
this poisonous mess
(a beautiful mess?)
God, where is the light?
where is the purpose?
where is my escape?!
-SAVIOR-
I have been consumed
fallen flat on my face
"double jeopardy."
all of these mistakes
leave me barren
lonely
DESTROYED
and all I have is you
but I am stuffed
brimming, with strain
father make me real again

father, help me feel again
oh, but this liquid
takes me away
a few precious moments
(several poisonous moments)
of feeling sane
and the smoke dissapates
where has everybody gone?
wont they return
to wrap me snug
inside a cleansing, holy white
"shes a danger to herself"
so self destructive
SOMEBODY SAVE ME FROM HER
and all he wanted was a brain
all he wanted was a heart
he just wanted to feel courageous
and the, SHE JUST WANTED TO GO HOME
"show me how to get back there
im so lost"
(he is chained ....)
scarecrows in the night, sadly prayed.

⟫HEART SMILES⟪ 1/2/06

it is too rare
that my heart ⟫SMILES⟪
it is too rare
that the corners of my lips
BEG. (...)
to touch my ears
so rare
yet, that is what gives beauty
to those that are endangered
it is those few
unexpected
moments
that lift EVERYTHING inside of you
and recharges your battery
curiosity raises its head
(or perhaps it is merely my LEVEL mind)
and wonders, as it searches desperately,
DEFENSIVLEY!
"why?"
"Oh! i dont deserve this!!"
listen closely dear friends,
THAT IS WHAT A GIFT IS.

and is not the greatest gift
one that is most UNDESERVING?
for, if it is deserving,
is it not expected? (what gift is that?)
BUT I ...
I want to cling to it
greedily DEVOUR it (yet..)
DENY it
at the same time
I'm afraid I am hopeful I am
a TEARY SMILE
wrapped in a defensive, forceful (loaded)
frown. PLEASE !!

PROVE ME WRONG look past it.
because
oh! I want to TRUST
I want so badly to feel this again
and.
           again.
AND.
         AND AGAIN !!
I want it like a spoiled brat in a toy store.

no.
I want it like an orphan
wants a HOME
I want it like
a caterpillar
longs for its *wings*
I WANT IT LIKE AN ADDICT
WANTS TO BE SOBER
THANK YOU

I would say it a million times
if it would convey how much it means
and im carried away
I want to explain   and explain
AND EXPLAIN.   AND EXPLAIN
and I wonder (what its like) (for you)
~~much more~~ how does it feel (for you)
is it like
chewing food
until it is void of all flavor
does it Rot the Mystery?
or am i serving you the answers

on a pretty (blunt) platter
my mind races
like mice
like rabbits
in every possible (and improbable, direction)
BECAUSE I WANT YOU TO UNDERSTAND.
you gave me
what I thought
I couldnt have
you dug beneath the dirty surface
and sought the root
I would not wish (like) to compliment myself
but how does a flower exist (grow, TOUGH)
without a dirty foothold
(no, it is not a foothold, BUT...)
IT IS THAT DIRT
THAT WHEN WATERED
WITH SUNLIGHT
that cause the flower to bloom
and grow
AND become desirable
to the observer

EVEN
to the most casual onlooker
I AM
THAT ORPHAN
I AM
THAT FLOWER

I AM

that observer
AND YOU.

HAVE. GIVEN ME.

WHAT. I LACKED.

thank you. thank you. thank you.

THANK YOU

for...

giving me what I lacked
what i was missing
for seeing me, and giving me HEART
SMILES.

i am stuck in a vicious cycle i am

1/7/06

did you know
your words are daggers
wrenching free
frozen (forbidden forgotten) tears
~~frozen~~ so hot
so cold
so fiery
                    they
                              BURN
everything inside of me as
            they fall
WHY

            what happened to family
                    to you
who are you now?
                    WHERE HAVE YOU GONE
and did i even know you
YOU HURT SO BAD
(pussy) crybaby, stopit stopit!!
STOP CRYING (stop feeling) ...i cant
how does this hurt so much   please
someone ease the pain (something?...)

and.... i cant (help it)
I DONT UNDERSTAND
    atleast give me that
broken windows   broken mirrors and
the shake and grinding teeth and
the WANTING yearning
in the asshole politely pleading
numb me numb me please
because
your words
are
DAGGERS.
                    and.....
                        im sorry?
                        love you?

Between The Trees*

@ MONICA'S BIRTHDAY PARTY

ERIN

April
(NO BRACES!!)

"I love veggies!!"

Fingertips
for a birthday
present...
- 5 DOLLARS
- FOR ME!!

JORDAN

RYAN

I dont know where to start   2/3/06
broken hearts
~~sad~~ little stories that (ssssSSh!!)
should never be told
THEY'RE TOO HORRIBLE TO BE TOLD. ....
my eyes wish a million times
to unsee what they saw
and too many viruses
system shut down
(there's no cure for that,)
THAT FILTHY HOT TUB
the VIOLATED
crippled, maimed, destroyed and mostly
DISTURBED
sit, sedated in harsh metal cages
and watched
bh!!the watching!!
dreadful boy (HE IS THE ANIMAL)
I caught him watching
greedily ravaging the scene before him
with those lustful beastly eyes
My heart is DISGUSTED with my eyes

too curious
no,
too unwise
they did not know any better
and I cant take it back
the shameful act
all recorded and branded
into my unsuspecting mind
OH!! AND TO BE TOUCHED
BY MY 'OWN HANDS'.... ITS....
AS IF I HAD VIOLATED MYSELF!!
there are no words to describe
the complete, unbearable HUMILIATION
the devastating EMBARASSMENT
in being attacked by youre own kind
HOW THE FUCK DO I DEAL
WITH THAT? I dont know how
I dont know how...
I FUCKING
CANT.

I cant I cant I cant I cant

HOW? HOW THE FUCK DO I HANDLE THAT?

No, I wont

(shake my head, my head begins to shake

I am loosing my composure

and the shaking

the heartful cries wrenching from the pit

of my wounded soul

the rocking

the *FEAR*

YOU ARE ALL ANIMALS NOW !!

I hate you I hate you I hate you I hate you

I hate that you understood my heart

because my hair

I hate the space you haunt

behind my eyes

the AWKWARD silence

while friend became foe

because friend? GET OUT!!

and you cry,

you have no where to go

ITS NOT MY PROBLEM.

then why do I care?!
IM SO CONFUSED.
and for the first time I
truly wish that I would die
and there is NOTHING to make it better
to ease the pain
and I am running
                    and hiding
                              crying.
SCREAMING
        AND
              SHAKING
                    rocking
THE BABY CURLED UP   retracted.
  ON THE CONCRETE
  the baby that wont be quieted
                    wont be consoled
and then I found my friend.
        swallowed several of them
flirted with the silence of forever
and escaped in a blank sleep
desperately clenching onto the hope of something
                                        better.

— APRY 3/8/06 —

* INCLUDE GOD IN EVERY ASPECT OF YOUR
LIFE. .... when alcoholics go out
and drink, the first thing they
leave behind is God.
(GIVE GOD 100%, not everything BUT,
absolutely everything.)

LET GO.

.... If you pray, dont worry
    if you worry, dont pray!
God is big enough to handle it and
He doesnt need my help.

— Lord, let him know there is POWER
            in prayer. Thank you.

— O.P.A.Y — 3/9/06

God, Grant me the serenity to accept the
things I can not change, the courage to
change the things I can, and the wisdom
to know the difference.

* "I learn that honesty is truth and
that truth shall make us free!" pg. 218
    — OUR SOUTHERN FRIEND

* Going somewhere else doesn't fix our problem,
our addiction, our problems, follow us. We
must deal with them here and now.

* "We never graduate from our disease"
* "ONCE AN ALCOHOLIC, ALWAYS AN ALCOHOLIC."

BAND MARINO @ BackBooth

with David, Jamie, $\frac{3}{8}$ Ashley
ran Christina ₁
$\frac{3}{1}$ Matt from Pita Pit

CRAZY dance PARTYS

tHe PatioNy

pita pit!!

SSSSUBER!!

Good Night Jamie tour

TASTE o7 CHAOS
AS I LAY DYING
THRICE
DEfTones
.... On Stage!!
w/ Jamie, David and Drew

"New Rule, you cant take any guys home
Renee!! " - Jamie "

I'm Nic'n !! PULL OVER!!

FUCK MYSPACE
9IRl

STomp BoYs

.... NICE EYES ....

" I'd like to fuck
her space.."

ROCKSTAR
energy drinks

THIS TOO SHALL
PASS....

As long as I'm not holding
on to it.

things will not always be this way.

FEAR KNOCKED ON THE DOOR
FAITH ANSWERED
AND NOBODY WAS THERE.
(When I have faith, there is nothing to
fear, God is in control.)

There is nothing a drink or a drug can make
better in this world.

THANKFULS:

5/1/06 1. My parent's joy in my life 2. The BEST night of my life last night 3. The opportunity to have a good job 4. My sponsor 5. My sobriety

5/2/06 1. Seeing Lisa pick up her 20 year medallion 2. Seeing Laura 3. I get to work tomorrow 4. A good meal 5. Fun w/ the girls on the van.

5/3/06 1. I STARTED WORK 2. God protecting me on the bus ride there, alone!! 3. Feeling competent 4. JAMIE 5. The love & support of others (TO WRITE LOVE ON HER ARMS)

5/4/06 1. I work tomorrow 2. Getting a bus pass 3. D helping me through a 'moment' 4. A walk 5. No new scars on my arms

5/5/06 1. Talking w/ Joy 2. Riding w/ Tyrell 3. A GREAT DAY AT WORK 4. My music 5. Coffee!

5/6/06 1. Going to a meeting w/ Ginger 2. Starbucks " 3. I'm where God wants me 4. A new person in my network 5. My job & my family, SOBRIETY

5/7/06 1. STATUS 2. lunch w/ my family 3. Erin 4. Kittens 5. Layla & Tyrell got baptized!!

5/8/06 1. Going to work 2. Phone cards 3. decent house mtg 4. A new counselor 5. Not getting bad consequences.

4/18/06

God works in mysterious ways.
I thought I was finally going job
hunting today w/ Keisha but it didn't
work out. At first I was so disappointed
and let down, I was frustrated and
angry & restless but I trusted that there
was a lesson and let go. Then this
evening things fell into place & now I
get to go tomorrow with Layla. I feel
like God was testing me to see how I would
handle the situation when it didn't work
out how I wanted. I think I passed.
Sometimes things happen differently than
you plan, & you just have to trust
that there's a reason, IT'S NOT ALL ABOUT YOU.
Christina helped me learn how to cook
Happy Joe's today, & felt SO good to
see everyone enjoy a meal that I cooked. I
felt so proud and happy!! I want to
cook for my family some day... I
have unanswered phone calls today and

It feels so wonderful to have moved up in the world at LMH. "movn on up, ♪ movn on up ♫" I need to remember that things fall into place all in God's timing. Acceptance is the key to all of my problems today. God has helped me kick off the weights of complacency and get working on my recovery again. I had quit journaling & working the steps and complacency is a major warning sign for me. But, I prayed for that to change and gradually it has. Thank you father. Aubee is in the hospital (day 2) and I'm worried. I've heard rumor she is getting kicked out. I hope she's ok. TRACY'S BACK!! She looks good, I'm so glad she's safe & she is here. Lord please guide and protect all those who have left. I lift up Amanda, please comfort her in her pain, be her shepherd, her rock, her refuge. Love her father bless her, keep her close to you.

Comfort, guide, and protect
the girls in this house,
show them there is a better
way to live, give them hope
for something better. Thank
you for the opportunity to
start over with my life.
Thank you for taking back
your prodigal daughter w/
open arms, I love you.
Please make me a shining star in
the universe. Give me eyes to see,
ears to hear & a heart to understand.
Hold Lora close to your heart,
comfort her, mend her broken
heart, show her your love, work
in her life. your will, not mine,
be done.

THANK YOU.

THANKFULS

5/9/06 1. Getting to work extra days 2. Coffee & cig's
3. Almost 2,000 friends on myspace 4. The support I have
5. My sponsor

5/10/06 1. Making it home in time 2. Fun at work
3. Photobooth 4. Writing Thrice 5. My new life

5/11/06 1. The weeks almost over 2. Kelly helping me w/
my fears about the root canal 3. That I have the
opportunity to even have a root canal 4. I'm clean &
sober 5. My mother

5/12/06 1. GETTING MY HAIR DONE - FREE!! 2. Austin and
Tricia 3. BOBA!! 4. A good day at work 5. Joy

5/13/06 1. Going to Cornerstone 2. All the shirts we sold
3. The support I have 4. Seeing my brother & Becky
5. All the band's support 6. Free clothes 7. dancing 8. Tea!!

5/14/06 1. A ride to the mtg 2. A good mother's day
3. Having the family together 4. Taco Bell 5. New shirts

5/15/06 1. A good day at work 2. Starbucks 3. someone to
walk home with 4. I didn't cut myself 5. My support
that keeps me accountable.

5/16/06 1. All the comments to my blog 2. Getting to work
3. Not missing the bus home 4. A good dinner
5. My music 6. Dustin from Thrice 7. Victory

THE LITTLE·RED BOOK

- PRAY - 9/19/06

* "...Trouble invariably begins with neglect of prayer. It slowly matures as they abandon conscious contact with God and service to others." pg. 103

* "...ask God for a changed circumstance after you have acknowledged and expressed thanks for your present circumstance."

* "Prayers of gratitude are especially good for alcoholics. They kill egoism and awaken us to life's true values."

* A CURE FOR THE 'RUT':

1. Cooperation with my Higher Power
2. Maintenance of my relationship w/ God
      NOW?

   - Simple prayers of sincere gratitude -

* "Pray for a renewed interest 'n' Prayer & in my relationship with God."

The First Sunday of May — STATUS with Tyrell?

THANKFULS —

5/17/06 1. Beginning to build a relationship w/ J.K Swift

2. Laughter 3. The opportunity to learn from my mistakes

4. My Music 5. God working incredible miracles in my life

5/18/06 1. Talking to Erin 2. The love and support of

my family 3. The relationships I have w/ my roomies

4. Being able to get feedback from Kelly

5. A comfy bed to sleep in.

5/19/06 1. Getting mail from Nana 2. New clothes

3. The growth in the Myspace account (over 2,000)

4. Getting to work 5. Sharing in a meeting

5/20/06 1. Going to Central 2. Fun on the van

3. A good mtg at Winter Park Group 4. Seeing Christine

5. Hanging w/ J.K Swift ☺ 6. Bonding w/ roomies !!

5/21/06 1. Pizza Hut pizza 2. A good time w/ my

sister 3. Erin's encouragement & wisdom 4. Cigarettes (B-day)

5. Joe D. getting to be w/ her sister 6. Kelly

5/22/06 1. Kristin's birthday, & her vulnerability

2. Patages (talk & hug) 3. THE KITTENS 4. God's protection

5. God using my story 6. The encouragement through the Myspace

SOMETIMES I JUST WANT
TO SCREAM !!!!

At this fucking disease
the damn URGES.
At the fact that I will always
have to fight
Sometimes I wonder what it would be like
to live without addiction
just.   to live.
But I know I wasn't meant
for simplicity
I was meant to fight
and scream and.
bleed.
Sometimes you have to live loud
to be heard.
I picture myself standing on the beach
clenching my little fists
beating them against
the big harsh world
laughing at me in the waves

And sometimes Overwhelming
likes to ride piggy-back on my weary shoulders
I sense her coming, feel her breath
on the back of my neck
and cry
Sometimes Maintanance
is merely a word.
And pink clouds are something
to abhore
I like mine gray and pregnant
with a thousand angry raindrops
a thousand purposeful tears
Sometimes I wish that 'why'
was somehow worth asking
Because I think I want to understand
the reason, the pattern
in picking and choosing
the who's who's and what's whats
and how it all works out in the end
AND SOMETIMES I JUST WANT
TO RUN
AWAY

from everything
I have to face
and seek out my comfortable numbness
Sometimes I wear familiar
as if it were my skin.
But then the mirror hates me and
I cant bare too see myself
the old must pass away
and a new life shall begin.
AND.
Sometimes I realize
that "Sometimes" is the spawn of fear
and rage is harming me
So I wrap myself in faith
and lie down in the moment
wait for it to pass and
just stay right here.
(and sometimes its okay to sceam.)

4/26/06

Once again I find myself falling behind. MAINTANANCE – so simple, yet so hard to do. Life gets hectic and I forget to make time for myself. Its funny how being on bedrest it'd be hard to find "me-time"...

I'm so grateful for my family, loving me, and trying to understand and support me through everything. I remember someone telling me once that family is something you come to appreciate later in life; not to take them for granted. I understand that now, I truly cherish them. Last night was the first time I've ever been up Even sober, and it felt SO GOOD. My heart was SWELLING up joy. All I could do was just snuggle up as close as I could and cry. I love her so much. I'm so thankful she stuck by me so patiently & lovingly through my active addiction.

I love that she never made me her "project", she was truly just there for me as a friend. She did everything because she wanted to, because she loved me. "HOW COOL IS THAT?!"

I'm learning to take care of myself. To rest when I'm tired, eat & drink when I need to, and pay attention to my feelings; deal appropriately w/ them.... wow, what a crazy concept!

Amber's gone. It was a long time coming. I'm relieved as awful as that sounds. I don't have to worry like that anymore. God protect her, comfort & heal her & her family, especially her little boy Cameron.

Sometimes I daydream about calling Grant or Zack and letting them know I'm ok. Sometimes I really miss them. But I have to let go of them & trust God will

give them back if he wants them
in my life. I can see & speak to
them in those quiet fairytale worlds
inside my head, & there I say
goodbye & they know I love them
and they're getting better so we
can all be together, but then I
leave them there and come back
to "earth". Sad. So, sad.

LET GO.
Of job hunting for now.
Of my things at the apartment, of
the friends that use, of
material things I can't regain
of my plans for the future, of
everything that troubles me,
and admit that I am powerless.

ACCEPTANCE
    IS THE ANSWER TO
        ALL OF MY PROBLEMS.
            ♡

HOUSE MEETING

* Memorial Day - Who's coming?
What are they bringing?
* Unity Weekend - 26th & 28th
(find how much money to spend: up to $15)
* June 12th Graduation (Lisa)
* June 3rd picnic
* P3 June 9-10-11th (evening of 9th)

5/28/06   THANKFULS
1. Jenny talk w/ Ashley 2. Spending time
w/ my family 3. Even taking my favorite
kitten home 4. A good urge 5. Picking up
my 90 day chip 6. Self-restraint
5/29/06 1. Seeing my family 2. New shoes
3. Good food 4. Xmas videos 5. Movie time
5/29/06 1. My sponsor 2. Spending time w/ my
family 3. Sarah deciding to stay 4. A good
book 5. Clean clothes
5/31/06 1. Music 2. I'm clean & sober 3. My
daddy 4. My sponsor calming me down
5. the ability to control myself
when I really wanted to hit
someone, & just walk away.

Mathew 18:10-14

Purpose (for the Pain)   4/27/06

I threw the stars across the sky for you
and one fell
like 1 tear from my eye
as you dropped to the floor
buried in the darkness and the lies

6/1/06 .

*Y*esterday is *history*,

TOMORROW IS A mystery,

Today is a GIFT,
(That's why they call it "the present".)

A VISION FOR YOU
pg 151

* VERY powerful,

4/29/06

I always have beautiful speeches in front of the silent (and oh so vulnerable) audiences in my head at night before I drift to sleep. This true I suppose I should write it down instead of letting it go to waste...

For the past several days I have been experiencing (I say 'experiencing' instead of 'having' because they are so vivid) these traumatic nightmares. Last night I dreamt I slit my throat and wore a scarf all day. The night before my ears were infested with tiny cockroaches and I was too afraid to touch them the entire next day. Still the night before that I dreamed I was eating pills. I was aware but still dreaming & was convinced evil ham was in my blanket and threw it across the room. It is just past my sixty days & I went through similar trauma during my thirty. 'Cocaine bugs' terrorize my body as I try to fall asleep. I hallucinate patterns & things and faces

and everything seems as if to be breathing,
fluctuating, rippling like waves away from
me. I have vivid flashbacks. Its as though
my life has been recorded in a series of
photographs, clippings, short films and
videos which play themselves at any given
time. I am watching me ....

Me, tripping on shrooms, staring at my
big beautiful pupils in the bathroom
mirror falling in love. Red lipstick
modern black haired Monroe - princess -
fairy. Just staring. Magnetic black holes,
so incredibly open. frozen. timeless.

Me, blowing up, the tingling chills
up my neck and the side of my head
and the hot cramping in my back.
and the dialated eyes, unavoidable.
vulnerable, festatic, euphoric, and oh so
deep.

Me, fragile and broken and empty
and bleeding and lost and STUCK
, ... and, its beautiful to me, so beautiful.

I envision brokeness, a very breakable little porcelain girl with scarred up wrists, salty eyes and an empty stomache. She's on the floor with tattered wings and frail eloquent flowing clothes. Ballerina legs and dark messy hair. She is seen only by certain hearts that can. Melancholy, there is something so very attractive and so fantastic about melancholy.

•*¸.✶´¨SAD AND BEAUTIFUL¸.✶*•

There is something so lovely about brokenness. I'm so drawn by distraction. Perhaps because I have been broken my whole life.

Perhaps it is because I know destruction intimately. Because maybe I am the destroyed. ("Once was?")

And maybe there is something hopeful that comes with being broken.

The hope that it can be fixed.

New.

And perhaps brokenness speaks of second chances

I have always been stuck on hope.
June Carter Cash is staring at me on the big screen telling me this is my second chance at life.

A picture of me in my yellow shirt my sunken boney frame hunched over about to do a line.

Me sitting on the bridge with my daddy's swiss army knife (slashing, digging, slicing). Fast foreward. and. My mommy and sister with mangled hearts, blurry vision, cleaning the blood. The screams. He tries to fix me. Panic.

Red lit up bathrooms and vomiting into the toilet while the innocent stand by gawking, horrified.

Me, the obedient slave. degraded. dirty. flawed and disgusted; too numb to care.

Another video and I am breaking into her 'open' house and simply going away.

The insanity of "going away".

Me in a flooded car in the ditch,
sideways at night. Dancing in my
twirly skirt and cowboy hat with a
cap gun in the middle of the road.
 And we were family.
WE WERE LIVING IN NEVER, NEVER LAND.
 Raking sand across his yard in my
underware while his greedy animal eyes
watched every move and the drinks,
oh how I drowned myself in the drinks.
Sometimes I can smell the sickly sweet smell
of burning cocaine.
 (Me, and Ryan sitting on the porch in
sunglasses smoking as the sun came up)
Sometimes EVERYTHING tastes like alcohol.

 I would never want to go through
this ever again and, yet,
I wonder at times if it will ever
stop.

IT IS SUCH A DARK & HORRIBLE MONSTER.

A MONSTER THAT WOULD LOVE TO TASTELESSLY
DEVOUR A RARE BUTTERFLY.

Teen gully, I am little and horrified.
Sitting on the dock while he sings me a song
he wrote about yours-truly.
I hate that he has a memory there.

Me, all alone crying, shivering, as I
sleep on the concrete forgotten, homeless.
wet and helpless (and STUBBORN?!)

My eyes rolling back into my head
the party surrounds me on the couch as I
overdose and they will throw my little
lifeless body in the lake.

The psych ward layout. A flood of
unpleasant smells, severe confusion, withdrawl
♪ You are my sunshine, my only ☉.
sunshine, you make me happy when
skies are blue...♪   ♫

Me, making out with ▓▓ on the floor
in our bathing suits dripping from the
cold shower and covered in smeary
glowstick and music I could feel.

THREE MEN IN SKI MASKS RELENTLESSLY
BEATING ME IN THE NECK & HEAD & RIBS.
MY NECK 'SNAPPING'. THE DELAYED PATHETIC
GROAN ESCALATING TO A HORRIFIED, DESPERATE
WEARY SCREAM "OH, GOD."...

VIKIDENT.

Bonfires and meteor showers and
getting lost in the twilight
zone with Ross.

Late night talks with Geoff. "Illegal"
cigarette breaks. Indie flicks. French horror
films. CRASH. His quiet nasaly voice. Big
pointy nose, sheltered from the sun. And
long blonde hair and black shirts and
Tori Amos. Music sample hours in my
apartment and coffee and sleeping on the
couch. A few true friends and poetry
shares and mix cd's and critiques.

Katie and smoking cloves and the
hurricanes.

Me, high at University in the courtyard
trying to use a payphone thinking I'm a washing
machine.

███████ cousin & brother trying to tag team with me. Her brother. Forceful. Truth or dare. and him making me watch him put on her clothes. Long walks through her neighborhood at night making up crazy dances.

Me, left in a ditch in the woods passed out.

And I wonder if composing these pop-ups on paper will relieve, help, delay, at all?

Morphine. sitting on my loveseat. nauseous. agitated. I hate everyone. Don't talk. But don't leave me alone. I'm scared. I'm going to die. Unable to move. Relaxed. Vomiting.

I'm so high. laying on the floor talking and laughing to/at myself uncontrollably. eight or nine blunts passing in the pow-wow.

HER taking advantage of me in the hot tub. trying to rip off my underwear in ███████ room. HIM lying on the floor watching them fuck; masterbating on the floor

I WANT TO SCREAM IT ALL AWAY
AS IF THEY WERE ALL BAD COLORS WHEN
I WAS TRIPPING.

And I don't even know where my speech was
destined. Ive tangled myself up in the
sticky web of my memories. They are
like thousands of pits of sinking sand.
sucking me in and filling me up,
heavy, drowning.
        ("The princess bride ... who shall
save me?")
My eyes grow weary and the sooner I
sleep the sooner tomorrow may come.
        (And now I lay down and anticipate,
"what dreams may come".)

GOD IS SO GOOD.   4/30/06

I cant even begin to fathom all that God is
doing with my life and in my life.

EVERYTHING IS COMING TOGETHER SO
VERY PERFECTLY.

I'm excited to wake up in the morning
Ive never smiled so much in my entire life.
My face hurts!!
My heart is SWELLING with pure joy.
("against such things there is NO law")

THRICE   COPELAND   ANBERLIN
                              SWITCHFOOT

* Thrice's singer is doing a solo project and
is writing a song about me "To Write Love on Her
Arms"
* Anberlin wears the shirt at every show
* Aaron Marsh from Copeland wrote me a letter
* Bands are "eating up the shirts"
Jayne wants me to work for him at HURLEY
making $10 an hour!!
People are calling me their hero....
Nathan Akers just hugged me and cried

Lizzie carried the burden of my addiction on her shoulders, dear sweet Lizzie....

God spoke through me tonight at STATUS — oh, to God be the glory.

I am a BLESSED VESSEL.

GOD, YOU ARE SO MUCH BIGGER THAN I AM.

"for I know the plans I have for you," declares the Lord, "plans to prosper you, not to harm you, plans to give you hope, and a future."

I cling to that promise.

He truly answers prayer.

GOD, MAKE ME A SHINING STAR IN THE UNIVERSE. LET ME NEVER FORGET, THIS IS ALL ABOUT YOU. GIVE ME EYES TO SEE, EARS TO HEAR, AND A HEART TO UNDERSTAND. THANK YOU FOR ALL YOU HAVE DONE, ALL YOU ARE DOING NOW, AND EVERYTHING YOU ARE GOING TO DO.

I'm so grateful that I know where I'm going when I die. I'm grateful that I'm free, and new, and YOURS.

I'm grateful for the overwhelming LOVE and SUPPORT of friends and family. The community, FAMILY, at STATUS. For the BEAUTIFUL new life God has given me. For Ryan's tattoos. Specifically for Jamie and David, Erin, Matt, Sedoni, Sanny, Nathan, Ashley, Daniel, and Josh lovelace, and AJ. May you completely refresh those that have refreshed me. Bless them beyond their wildest dreams. Thank you for placing Christy ███████ in my life. Strengthen and comfort and bless her in her recovery as well.

I'm thankful for Starbuck's Mocha Frappccinos, and Lucky Strikes and my cd's, & new shoes.

MY HEART IS FILLED WITH SONG TODAY. I am a constant 'WORK in progress'. Continue to refine me, mold me into the person you created me to be. Help me to keep my head up when it floods & keep my eyes on YOU.

I'm thankful for Aebys.

God, please prepare the one for me, and
prepare me for him. Let it be a union that
glorifies you. (Wah, & can it be ████████ please?! ")
WOW. I just can't fathom
your beautiful plan.
Thank you for choosing me.... WOW.

THANK YOU FOR THIS DAY.
It was the best day of my life....
THANK YOU.
            Thank you.

Thank you.   thank you.
                            Amen.

— Laura's AA study — 5/4/06

* Part of my destructive behaviors are due to my disease

* Most AA's can't recover on their own — I need a program

* Is my life becoming unmanageable in my recovery?

* I need to remember my "bottom"; remember the nightmare, & get desperate, serious about my recovery. Do I want to live??

* What am I powerless over?
  1. My thoughts
  2. Other people's decisions & perceptions
  3. My disease

* While I may be powerless, I do control how I act/react to that which I am powerless over.

* Am I experiencing an emotional hangover?
  1. Take inventory   2. Make peace
  • Spot √ — spontaneously through day
  • Days End — review inventory of the day
  • Balance — see how things weigh out
  • Progress — check progress w/ others

* Inventory should be a regular, day to day event, fundamental assett of maintaining a spiritual program.
* Wether resentment is justified or not it is always detrimental — spot check
* LOOK FOR PROGRESS NOT PERFECTION
* Practice restraint, avoid sulking & isolating,
♪ Oh, Let my pride fall down ♪
* Growing up is a painful progess (GROWING PAINS)
* 11th STEP PRAYER
* Do unto others as you would have them do unto you.
* Check your motives
* Beware of the enemy: RATIONALIZING
* honest regret, genuine ~~attitude~~ gratitude, & willingness are assets we shall gain
* When Im disturbed, something's wrong w/ Me
* The success I have is HIS not Mine, it is only by the grace of God I am sober today.

for the first time in a while I had the
urge to cut myself last night.
I see the patterns   and
everything seems to happen by default.
(How can you prevent that?)
I'm so frustrated!! I dont understand
why I must constantly be the lab rat
why change is always taunting me
why I even bother asking 'why.'
I dont know what to do
("So, do nothing at all," whispers the voice
inside my head)
I sit on my bed and all I can do
is weep and scream one awful word
over and over I cry, "NO".
No - I dont want to cut
No - not again,
I cry out in dismay, in honor, and
in awe ...
     How has it come to this again?!
Where did I go wrong.

No - a small child being pushed to
the edge of a cliff....
No - I envision little Anne w/ her red
hair ontop of the bridge her pursuer
quickly gaining as she finds herself
cornered w/ no apparant way to
escape. She is faced w/ the option of
jumping ? plumenting to her death
or allowing her assailant to catch her
And just then, rescue comes from
out of the dark and carries her off
to safety. WAIT FOR THE MIRACLE.
"No", a cry for help,
and as the music eased my restless
soul rescue became possible through
the attentive ears of my roommate.
Thank You God.

GREEN HOUSE   5/6/06

* When I enjoy conflict & beating other people up, its because I am beating myself up. There is something wrong w/ <u>me</u>. It is my disease —

* DIS-EASE, when I am in my disease, I like to make others the same
  "misery loves company"

* <u>What's going on w/ me?</u>

* Ask God to reveal the problem, pray for ACCEPTANCE, ask him to remove it.

* I think like an Alcoholic/Addict with or without drugs in my system.

— Drugs are just gasoline on the fire
  (the fire is ALWAYS there)

* <u>REMAIN TEACHABLE</u> — there is always more to learn. when I think I've got it all, IM IN TROUBLE!!

* Every struggle I make it through w/o picking up is a chance for me to GROW.

* Approach life as a Learning experience (HUMOR)

East Side   5/6/06

UNDERSTANDING

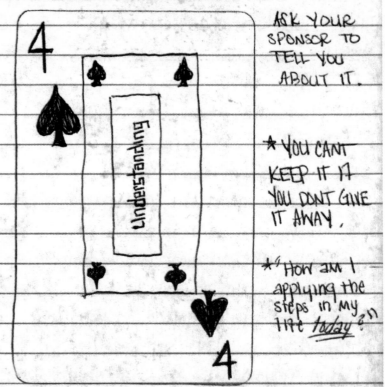

4

Understanding

4

ASK YOUR
SPONSOR TO
TELL YOU
ABOUT IT.

* YOU CANT
KEEP IT IF
YOU DONT GIVE
IT AWAY,

*" HOW AM I
applying the
steps in my
life _today_?"

Isolation is
detrimental to
MY RECOVERY.

* _The importance of change_

* Get used to CALLING people for help.
(I need to get outside of myself.)

* Dont try to explain the unexplainable

* I want to know _WHITNEY_. ⊂ depression
                                 isolation

1 STATUS
— Truth about Tjroids — 5/7/06

* Lawlessness does not promote freedom
(it promotes chaos)

— In Judges they'd taken 'truth' into their
own hands because they had no God

TRUTH — must be UNIVERSAL
and UNCHANGING.
IT CAN NOT BE RELATIVE.

* The decisions we make often enslaves us.
" HOW DID WE GET HERE?"

[Romans: Chpt 1:22-25] ...We lost the truth,
we removed ourselves from God's authority.

1. We become fools 2. Exchange truth & lies
3. Don't acknowledge God as authority
4. They knew truth — CALAMITY.

* Our choices are SO much bigger than us.

★ OKAY ★   5/21/06

* Half measures avail us nothing
* If nothing changes, nothing changes
* Be fearless & thorough
* If you want it, you'll get it
* Prayer is not a sign of weakness, it's a sign of strength
* It will only get worse each time I go out, this is a progressive disease
* Our dreams can come true in sobriety
* We can't make things happen, we have to let them / surrender our will
* We don't always have to learn the hard way, today we can learn from others' mistakes & take advice.

Unexpectedly I felt the world come
crashing down on my head
"Oh ... you FUCK UP" she sneered,
"You silly little FAILURE," I cry
you need to be PUNISHED   BUT
don't let them do it   you do it instead
AND IT HURTS!!

                    like a twinge in my heart
my soul is cringing
                    underneath the sting
                              of their words
(Or is it her words that are so painful?)
Everything fades to black
and fuck the white im dark and bitter and angry
          and confused
i want to paint heavy shadows on my eyes
and look deflated, sunk, hollow.... shattered
I WANT TO SLASH MYSELF TO PIECES
"NO!" nononono.... No.... OH GOD....
im afraid to ask for help
          a sad sick familiar part of me
                    doesn't want help.

It feels cozy hear, it begins to smile,
            get comfortable,
BUT ITS' SHARP AND VICIOUS AND.... pretty.
NO!!   all I can do is whimper,
shake my little head. "Hello, Panic!" she says,
"How've you been? I've missed you, glad
you're back clear!"
            ....No, not again.
I squeeze my stupid eyes shut.
        "No one CARES!!" that's not true..
"No one has come for you, you're sabotaged
EVERYTHING, AGAIN." Hot tears.
 Once more I shake my head in silent protest.
I fear Im losing control. "Stifle those tears
you PUSSY!!"   I hold my breath.
 ...dig my nails into my palm...
Scissors dance on the screen behind my eyes.
no.... A stiff old woman is brutally wringing
out my wet heart.
     I begin to shut down.
                autopilot.
                    declere.

"Make them think you're ok so they
leave you ALONE." She is so cunning.
.... Yes, ok, ok.
I am calm, cool, collected.
        black streaky face and all. and.
Ofcourse they fall for it.
.... no, please .... no..... no....
and a shower would be refreshing,
   you could shave your legs... wink, wink.
I am a soldier now.
I am a machine.

I am armed and dangerous.
                        (no!! no ....)
I stand there in the water and my eyes
are searching, searching.
My eyes are searching and they rest on my hip.
but, it looks so soft
                        and so smooth
  Oh!! PLEASE!! I just want to keep it.
  It looks so pretty and pure.
            PLEASE! I DONT WANT TO!!

"Stop being such a PUSSY and
DO IT!!" she screams breathlessly,
"Look, just FEEL it..."
I hold the RAZOR and stare hard at
the brand new blades. I . just . stare .
and . stare . ...
I WANT to. It's REALLY VERY SIMPLE
AFTER ALL. AND NO ONE HAS to KNOW....

My gaze falls heavily on my hip again.
I watch the water flow steadily, gently,
over it and down my thigh.
        I imagine it RED.
                            NO!!
BUT I WANT to.
                    I CANT.
I SIMPLY CANT. I CANT DO IT.
"What the HELL is WRONG with you?!"
she is desperate and so VERY angry.
"Just FUCKING DO IT, damn it, you
deserve it, you HAVE TO!!"
                BUT I CANT.

"Oh my God!" I CANT,
oh God.   OH God,
              I CANT.
And I see all of their words on the
screen. A crowd full of faces looking into
Mine. Watching, Hoping, Begging.
And I wonder what if Johnny Cash died
instead.   AND I JUST CANT.
I throw down the RAZOR and bang my
fist on the wall and just cry.
I weep with relief
     and CoNfusioN
              and Anger,

     but Mostly relief.

5/16/06

An ant
scorched, burning,
under the concentrated beam of sun
that has found him through the eye
of the magnifying glass.
I dont think he is wondering
why.
I dont think he is telling himself
"I deserve this".
And I dont think his little legs
are itching to harm himself
to distract him from the pain.
Smoke begins to curl upward
crackle, sizzle.
He is frying on the sidewalk
down by the road
he was traveling on.
I wonder if he has
any hope.
I wonder if he sees
a way out.

Or if he is going to give up
and die.
But wait!!
The beam shifts
just when all was lost
when his vulnerable insides were almost baked
A cooling breeze ran over him.
And I take heart as I realize
God will never give me more than I can take.

5/18/06

I really dont understand, but it's
come to my attention that the
reasons are not important, it's
a learning experience. This consequence
is teaching me so much; has given
me what I wouldn't have seen
otherwise.

I'm getting sick of petty
gossip and the "conspiracies"
happening on staff but I
know this time it's all about
me.

If I want to live, I can't
pick up again. ... it's a scary
thought. I feel like I'm
walking a tight rope and if
I slip; fall there is nothing
below to catch me... I will
die. God guide me in my
recovery.

5/19/06

It SUCKS. Seeing people who came in after me getting picked up for meetings while i have to sit here and ride on the damn van, Phase fucking one. UGH. I'm fine one minute (maybe because I forget), and the next I'm so rediculousely depressed and jealous and angry AND hurt. I hate emotional roller coasters.

damn it.

HOWEVER,

I did enjoy myself COMPLETELY playing pictionary with some of the girls since we have no T.V. pewileges. My team kicked some serious ass. ☺ Despite the utter CHAOS due to the fact that the people playing were a bunch of highly competitive addicts; we managed to have a great time.... those of us who won... haha.

✝ I'm thankful that we had no T.V so that we could enjoy each other. ♥

5/20/06

.... she said that she let her little girl take a shower alone w/ a man who had just gotten out of prison....

AND MY HEAD EXPLODED IN AN AWFUL DISPLAY OF FLASHING PICTURES.

They were so loud,

they ~~HURT~~.

█████ ~~taking me in the shower~~ I was drunk I was dying they had ganged up on me I was suicidal I tore my arms to fucking pieces and HE ....was my friend...

he was supposed to rescue me...

█████ ~~pushing me against the wall~~ as ~~the water runs in my eyes and I am a slave, I am obedient.~~

SHUDDER.

I HATE YOU.

I HATE YOU.

I HATE YOU!!!!

I HATE YOU.

I AM SLICING MY WRISTS IN THE BATHTUB.
A CIGARETTE BETWEEN MY LIPS. MUSIC. LOUD.
IT IS MY SYMPHONY. MY "INVITATION TO DANCE".
        The horror.
A shower is supposed to be somewhere
to get clean.

        I was made dirty in the shower.

Behind the feeble curtain I feel empty and
vulnerable and scared.
        DEFENSELESS!   ashamed.
behind the curtain my heart was slain.
and I want to cry and my insides ache
they want to scream and beat it out of me
but I shut down.
        my stomache twists into knots.
                I check out.
My eyes are black holes as they suck in the
contents of the room searching for anything
to distract, take away.
        I want something to relieve my pain.

My hands begin to shake,
palms are beaded with sweat.
He is watching me and I think he is
a pig....
On the van I sit and stare into the
silent summer sky and try to drift
away.
   but all I can think of is how much
   I hate.

5/21/06

I want to take you
and make you the bad guy.
I sit and cry because I
feel like I can't do anything right.
she wants a fairytale
and she wants to take
and break everything pretty.
she wants to die,
to hide inside the dark corners
of my mind and beat me.
I rock, back & forth; I'm coming unglued
and tear at my hair and
try not to care but it isn't true.
One minute I do and the next I don't
I want to stay and run
away and guard my heart
from anymore pain but I won't.
And it's all so confusing; I hate myself
and I'm not ready to try;
but I'll place you safe
upon the shelf
until the time is right.

5/12/06

Your white truck and Lucky Strikes
and driving fast with the wind
whipping my face and playing with
my hair and David Gray
and you sang,
you always sang....
AND YOU THROWING ME DOWN AND TAKING
MY PHONE AND WE ARE SCREAMING AND YOU
ARE AWEFUL AND IM AFRAID. AND THE RAGE....
We are fucking in your bed but you
wont kiss me because you said
it wouldnt mean anything.
On the boat an water so clear
and blue and I faced my
greatest fear and we laughed
and kissed and I liked you....
IM DRUNK AGAIN FROM THE LIQUOR YOU GAVE ME
AND YOU ARE ANGRY AND YOU ARE MY MASTER
YOU HOLD THE KEY IN THAT BOTTLE AND I
HAVE TO BEG FOR YOU TO GIVE ME ANY.
    Klonipin ....

And i want sex because everything
has lost its effect and you make me
please you first but you fall asleep
"Your damn medication" and i drown
myself in the bottle and i cut
myself, i bleed and try to run,
to flee, but you tackle me down
the stairs and carry me like a rag
doll back to my cage and tell
me to go to sleep.
YOU LOCK ME IN THE ROOM AND ITS
UGLY AND YOUR THROWING ME AROUND AND
YELLING OBSCENITIES AND SO AM I AND I
WANT TO DIE AND OH, ILL SHOW YOU,
AND IM SLASHING UP MY THIGH AS I
STARE INTO YOUR BEAUTIFUL BROWN EYES.
I eat two bottles worth of jello shots and
swallow some pills and agree to meet.
Youre 'so' condescending and you think
I must have forgot oh,
but i most certainly have not.
How could I?

IM SICK, SHAKING ON YOUR BED ...?

WITHDRAWING FROM MY 'BEST FRIENDS' AND

YOU ARE SHAKING ME YOU DONT CARE

YOURE ANGRY AT ME FOR MAKING YOU

LOOK BAD. (YOU MADE YOURSELF

LOOK BAD YELLING AT ME INFRONT

OF MY FRIENDS YOU BASTARD)

I AM HAVING SEIZURES AND I THINK I

AM DYING AND AQUA TEEN IS PLAYING

LOUD AND IM HALLUCINATING AND YOU

ARE LAUGHING AND BOUNCING THE

BED UNTIL I THROW UP. AND YOU

ARE MAD AT ME FOR BIENG SICK

AND I CANT SEE STRAIGHT AND IM

SO HURT AND FILLED WITH HATE.

BUT YOU ARE HITTING ME AND POKING

AS I LIE THERE HELPLESS.

You, buying me close to make up.

You. Paying for some fancy expensive

hair cut to make me forget.

you. driving 120 mph down the road

to scare me, and I am frozen.

You writing pretty words to make
it all better and stabbing your
fingers into my eyes so I won't cry
and you tell me about some other
girl that you love and I broke.
  You, acting like my dad.
YOU talking shit about my family,
and your beautiful dogs.
and soft towels and inviting smell.
Smoking weed and calling me a
fuck up for having a drink.
Us. shaking. locked away in
that crazy place and you were
my Knight come to rescue me and I
wonder what happened and what
the fuck was I thinking. . . . .

5/23/06

She was crying and I felt my heart

d
  r
   o
    p...

the guilt stirred up inside of me, tied
itself into an uncomfortable knot
an undeniable need for purging,
I had to force it all out of me,
all those secrets I wish I'd forgotten...
The unsettling silence
    then   the hands
shot up one by one
gagging on the seeds we'd swallowed
denying them the right to grow
forging new paths to walk on
we were bitter and sweet
filled with grief, heavy sorrow
and I hope and pray and trust
that something good will come of this
and I see her sinking

watch her shutting down
slipping away in our midst
I long to crawl
painstakingly, lovingly
to her and pull her back
but she is angrily building
her blind brick wall
I feel I am viewing
in slow motion
her dangling over the edge.
I am watching her fall,
Tears well up
spring forth from my eyes
I feel like it's my fault
and still....
the lies!!
The Murderous Masks
that we like to hide
behind....
Take them off!!
Cut the act!!
You are going to DIE!!

But she wont hear
and I have taken away
here only reason
the one thing
that made here stay
Oh but I know
that if you arent here for your
it isnt good enough
and if you arent ready
I wont hang on to you,
Oh, God, teach me,
the art of letting go.

5/29/06

It all goes **BLACK**.
I feel my heart sinking and sinking
an anchor plummeting
searching in the depths for
something
anything to hold on to
but I have found nothing
it is all slipping away from me
in the darkness that has fallen
heavy
and nearly complete....
children on the black top
holding cardboard cut outs
to watch the eclipse at their feet
And I am angry at God.
but, I must TRUST
I wrestle with the loss
lying on the floor
in silence
until a hand
His hand, reaches down

and gently plays with my hair
runs fingers through my scalp
the child begins to allow itself
to be soothed
"come here ... go away"
I allow myself to feel
the comfort
and my pain
banish the pictures
from my head
BROKEN and DEATH
have no place
on my arm
or
in my heart
it is unfamiliar to say no,
change my mind this late
I am relieved
and I know
I'll never have to bleed again
if I keep letting go.

5/25/06

My sponsor came today. She said I looked
different, not my usual self. Maybe it is
because I am changing. Maybe because I
am feeling very close to darkness and
struggling at the same time with this
foreign "light", and I am confused.
I told her about my actions & consequences
and losing my job. She said,
"Try saying that you gave it away."
...so I do, and it feels like shit.
It is taking ownership. It is humbling.
I hate it, but I do it....for me.
I know that work environment wasn't healthy
for me. This is all a change for the
better. CHANGE IS SUCH A BITCH. I
hate it. (what's new)
But I need to remind myself to
practice what I'm learning, apply it.
My words only go so far. ACTION. &
what really speaks.
        Your will, not mine, be done...

3/26/06

Pam's carrot cake is the most
amazing thing to ever rock the
world of LVH.

It felt like home, much like
my mother's....

Watching the countdown at   5/27/06
the convention sent chills down my
spine. I can't remember the last time I
felt so proud. I jumped up with my
arms triumphantly in the air when
they called out 90 days....

I saw Darla, a girl I went to HS with
at University. She was on JV soccer.
How small a world we live in.
Tyrell said she was very proud of
me for staying despite everything. & I
couldn't stop smiling.

Not to mention, I had a nice, lazy
day lounging around in my pj's
not doing any groups. Finished my
3rd step AND did Sunday. (2nd time ever)

5/28/06

"When I spoke at meetings I used to say that I was a scumbag piece of shit, but my sponsor said to stop, that it wasn't true, I never was those things, I JUST MADE SOME BAD CHOICES....

— speaker at OA AA

5/29/06

I felt like a child dropped off at daycare, screaming & crying, begging not to be left behind as I watched my family leave today. It was strange, and new, and awful, and good. Before I only missed or felt attached to my dog. I wonder how it felt when I left them. It must have killed their hearts....

5/30/06

IM FUCKING PISSED AND TIRED AND SO FUCKING THIRSTY AND THOSE MOTHER FUCKERS DONT FUCKING CARE. STINGY ASSHOLES. I NEED A FUCKING DRINK AND THEY WONT FUCKING GIVE ME ONE.... I HATE THEM. THEY ARE LIARS.!!!!

....and I love my dad

ENYA Meditation   5/31/96

There is a woman in a long twirly
white dress, running. It clings to her &
seems almost gray in the rain that is
pouring down, pulling her black mascara
down her cheeks. She has long, dark
tangly hair that falls in loose curls
on her back. She is running to a
man & the pain between them is
intense. She is sorry. She is grateful.
It's an intense scene as she locks onto
him and he is spinning her around
and around. The camera floats upward,
above them, spinning with them. It
is sad and beautiful. ...
Me, standing defeated in the kitchen of
my old apartment holding the phone in one
hand, an empty bottle in the other. It is
slow and heavy. It is raining inside. I
am screaming, "What the FUCK DO I DO?!"
Just screaming and crying, nearly in
shock. Yet, it is nearly a silent flick.

The pain is so loud I can hear it. The bottle drops and smashes on the floor. I have the razor and lock myself in the bathroom. I begin to carve, slow motion, FUCK UP on my right forearm. The music grows darker, more pressing, insistant, like my friends on the other side of the door trying desperately to get in.

Suddenly I see me lying on the bed in the dark while ██████ is raping me and his friend in the bed next to me is trying to make me suck his dick. We are jerking back and forth and his dick is on my face.

(I begin to shudder and cry in silent agony on the couch)

Then I am cutting myself and drinking and trying to hang myself.

I see me lying passed out on a couch my eyes rolling back into my head and I hear them say they will toss my body in the lake if I die.

Now I am on the bridge staining it
in dark pools of blood as I rip open
my wrists with my daddy's swiss army
knife.
I am Belle and then i am the Beast
and I can see the rose in the glass
case, wilting away.
Now Im collapsed on the floor, broken...,
And now I see me walking through
the halls at LMH for the first time.
My nose is bleeding.
I see david banging his fist on the
table outside while I smoke and stare
up at him through teary, bloodshot eyes.
I dont want to sign the papers.
Then, we are going back inside,
the music is hopeful, becoming more
lively each minute.
I am at the Magic game. Im watching
Thrice onstage. I smell cigarettes and coffee.
Now I am back at LMH. My body is
covered in black patchwork skin.

slowly I begin to dance, to feel,
and grow. Bit by bit little pieces
of black are removed to reveal pure,
beautiful white porcelain skin.
I can see the kittens and I am laughing.
I am forming new friendships and
snuggled up in a tangle of arms
with my family on the couch.
It is still sad, but it is transforming.
It is becoming more hopeful and
optimistic even still.
and then....
The music is gone. It has died.
Quickly faded away just as it came.
I see a little life-size ballerina in
the middle of a barren black room.
She stops dancing much too abruptly
Then she is moving backward with
long sweeping steps. Her movements
are exaggeratedly fast as though
someone had placed her in
"Rewind". She quickly steps back

into her music box and the lid
closes silently + purposefully, behind
her.
All is mute, blank, still as the hot
tears continue to make rivers
down my face and I wait.
I wait patiently for the instructor
to bring us back, open our eyes.
I wonder if I will tell them what
I've seen on the projectors
behind my eyes.....

A NEW LIFE

one day at a time...

1/16/07

She came to me
sent to me
in a withering carcass
skin hung on thin
wire hangers
eyes

WIDE

open.

THERE.

she wore my story
she brought it with her
and i felt God in my heart
choking on stories and
the truth
drained and sick ,
sat
there
ready to be

Simply be
what I am   in Him
for her.
And the reason, the purpose,
rang out so pure and true.

I can not save you.
(But He can, He can, and I
am a tool).
Why are n't called to be strong
when n't too weak?

My mind it jumps
from here to there
and in between I
feel things when I please
then leave it somewhere
out of reach
they swing
or do I?
kick and pull or push
it is posed to me
perhaps
I am all of these
and it makes me spin.
I hate you I love you
come here go away
BRAKE ME
am I not shattered already?
and there isn't enough space
to tell you where I am

I disagree with EVERYTHING I say
I feel stuck
where do I begin
there are so many pieces
to give
and I skip from parts of each
leaving nothing
of something behind
catch up
I've missed too many days I'm
failing
(FAILURE IS NOT FALLING DOWN
    ITS STAYING DOWN)
falling....
in a vast ocean of my thoughts.
the words escape me so often
I have lost them
in the smoke
in the fury of my fragile past

I HATE REACHING,
RETURNING WITH OPEN EMPTY PALMS.
you'd think after you leave
the fog behind you get
your vision back...
but you lose that too,
sifting through the debris
the wreckage
rebuilding from the scraps
splinters and exhaustion
blood, sweat, tears
and the joy in something NEW
you wear it everyday
until it is old and you long for
something else
foot holds and new chains and
treading
BEWARE!!

I need you to fix my

because I need it back...

1/19/07

What's wrong with me?
she says
I say, and I dont know
why I break my back
as they walk away
as I scream and run
when I want to stay
I keep you at a distance
fill my time
with schedules
appointments
not people....
there are so many
that I'm left alone
wondering why
and feeling safe or
afraid
I am the only constant
WHATS WRONG WITH ME?

my heart feels discarded
because no one holds it
Oh how nice it would feel
to be missed,
and sometimes or most times
I dont miss them.
I want someone to call
at three am
to lay here with me
and laugh or cry
or drive for hours
talking in beats and
melodies soaring between us,
through the windows with
the smoke
to teach me about laundry
and cooking and fleas and
life
to share mine with

share theirs
ours.
but I wont let it happen, oh!
WHAT is WRONG with me?
Volatile, he says
I say fucked up
would be a more tender way,
too balanced, that guy,
and I am five and
I want more
AND sometimes nothing at all.
Teach me about
BOTH AND

in this world of
EITHER OR

Its something my heart does not
YET comprehend

2/6/01

When did promises snap like twigs.
When did our words become
weightless and empty.
When did we get to this place
where we were so greedy.
I don't want to be here.

I DONT WANT TO BE HERE.

yelling at my dog (him)
laying in a filthy mess
feeling dead and vile and
numb and blank and
wanting so badly to tear my flesh.

I DONT WANT TO BE HERE.

blacking my eyes and
throwing up my food, dying
to go home and
sleeping on the floor.

' DINT WANT TO LIE IN
THIS FUCKING BED.

contaminated. dirty. tainted.
stained. destroyed. filthy.
filthy. filthy. filthy. awful.
stupid broken bed.

nor do I want you in it.
or anyone else.
   it would be wrong.
(who would want to?)

How did we get to this place
where scabs are never
given a chance to heal
where we pick and rip and
tear them at
Oh! Impatient world!

Sad, wretched little world
and how beautiful?!
filled with contradictions
complimentary
opposites.
How do you (co-) exist?
I DONT WANT TO BE HERE.

with this rotting carcass
of a monster sunk sharp
into my organs
refusing to lift
leave my insides
GET ME OUT OF
HERE.
LET ME THE FUCK
OUT.

MARIONETTE
I dance brainless through
the motions
one foot in front of the other
pleasing, appeasing
wooden and hollow and dying
to be free.

how do I heal?

when I want to starve
everything that feels.

I could wash these sheets a
million times and they would
NEVER be clean.

And I don't know anything,
anymore.

cushion her w/ music
a song to break her fall
a melody is a parachute
and a sledgehammer and
a bandaid and salt and
scalpel and a microphone
and a tear and something,
when we are nothing at all.

I DONT WANT TO BE
HERE.

used and useless and
oh so confused.
IM SO CONFUSED!!
is he just a dog
returning to his vomit
am I his VOMIT?
and he yelled at me
for thinking such things of his mess.

and he left me to clean it and
I DONT KNOW HOW.
I DONT KNOW HOW

to deal with this.
to clean this mess (WOUND)
to sleep again and
believe
this room can somehow
be new, and clean....

I DONT WANT TO BE
here.

if I lay down (in it)
I am frozen and stiff and still
mind racing, exploding
scattering, fragmented all
over the place, every place
but here.

My eyes fixed
through the cieling
Salty and bitter and beggung,
sweaty balled up fists
hoping desperately I
can squeeze hard enough
to drive my nails
into my palms
and then perhaps just focus
on that, because.

I DON'T WANT TO !!!!

be here.

tounge feels severed
and swollen
just a worthless lump
inside my dry mouth.
and I am choking on oranges.
I said no.

but he said she said i guess
the words get lost in the bullshit,
kicked up in the dust behind
us as we run.
was I the finish line?
Oh, but surely not "I"
as in my person, my
heart, surely "I"
as in my self, the
hateful thing I exist
in. ,...
and well I guess you won.
My body is
the spoils of war.
HOW DISGUSTING.
the plunder you ravaged and
claimed after forcing your
way through
tricky, scheming, lying

son of a bitch
what kind of victory is that?!
but I can't be mad
he cried.
and, cried
as I lay there concentrating
on being numb.
I NEVER SAID THAT WORD....
(he did, over and over again)
SHUT UP!! SHUT THE
FUCK UP!!!! I said I
didn't want to hear it I
didn't want to believe it.
and his tears made _me_
want to die,
how does that work?

how do you get to make ME
feel guilty?!
so
    I
        hold
            my
                breath.
        hold
            my
                tears.
                my
                    tounge.
this isn't something
you tell everyone.
I am rageful and irrational
filled with days
of retail therapy
and naps that eat the sunlight
soothe the ache

I lie (in my bed).
the ringing in my ears
but i choose not to hear
you.

          .... any of you.
I just stay here in this
blue color
that used to be red
pained by the reason.

and there's a bottle
in my fridge.
scissors on the counter.

THEY WILL NOT BE MY SOLUTION.

I CRY OUT IN the darkness
but NO ONE HEARS me.
I AM A CHILD

who has fallen and bruised
screaming, some pitiful wail,
whine, deep groan...
mommy! mommy!
I cry for my mother
and father to comfort
me, to be here w/ me.
but I have placed them
carefully
far from here.

this cut is one
their lips shall never meet.

As I ride silent in the car
I wonder through the possibilities
staring at my stomach.
No, I can't go there...
I can't go there...

BUT I DONT WANT TO BE
HERE.
this bad trip that I cant end
where nothing is what I want
it to be, where whoever im
with I dont want to be
with and I dont want to
be anywhere I am and
nothing is comfortable and
everything feels wrong.

I could be a million things.
a million alternate endings.

I could stop eating and stay
in bed. a hermit. alone and
mostly dead.

I could pretend this never happened

I could run all the time and
work and work and never
stop going and doing.

I could backslide and relapse
and just disappear for awhile.
or maybe I'd just out.

The healthy options are hard
to linger on.....so foreign.

Im constantly paranoid of
something aweful happening
to me.
One night im convinced my
right lung has collapsed.
The next my heart is going
to stop.
Im going to be kidnapped

and tortured.
Or become pregnant
and die giving birth.
Perhaps my dog is going to
turn on me and
latch on to my throat.

The Lord says He has
PLANS for me, to prosper
me, NOT TO HARM ME
to give me hope and a
future ....
   HOW DOES THIS FIT IN?!

no pain. no gain.
Current mood: distraught

you are sickly sweet and stunning.

untouchable.

and i am rotting silently in the corner.

dismissed.

invalidated.

with every finger wrapped around my cancer, pointing back at me. only me.

it was always only mine.

how do i teach my brain that you are not infallible?

i don't know how to be angry at you.

only rageful. only safe and unapproachable. only caged.

only angry on my arms.

oh, my arms,

they took every beating i could never give you.

all the blame, all the hurt, never had an outlet.

and today a rose has formed through the scars, built up from the healing

today my heart thought maybe it was pretty,

though you would never say it.

never see (it..me..my heart..my rose)

only the thorns, the cuts, how ugly it was. only my hands that did it all.

alone.

give me something!!

give me a name, a voice, a thing to put my finger on.

something to slash at.

other than myself.

but my heart is a distant whisper as you go

through your day, your surface, your clean house.

i'm not as dirty as you made me feel! and if we rub any harder you'll just rub me away.

right out of color, out of shape.

don't dismiss me!

LOOK.

at my story

painted so clearly for you, them, me...

but you close your eyes and speak of my teeth and what you wear.

it wears on me.

tonight. it breaks me down to small pieces. insignificant, indignant, pieces.

unravelled, unfamiliar and painfully aware.

amidst the switches

shutting my ache on and off in uncontrollable bursts.

i have to sit in a room seven days later to even see that it hurt me.

i spoke of _**love**_

and you watched tv

i poured out rivers on your counter

for the comments about my body

seeking reassurance, seeking peace,

and you gave me blame, fault, responsibility.

WHERE DO I TAKE THIS HURT?!!

the answers are so fuzzy and removed

so i curl into the softest, safest place i know, and sleep.

and dream. and plead.

and wait.

for healing.

knowing full well that i will have to hurt first.

and i think that's what scares me the most.

Friday, November 23, 2007

pretty houses and heavy hearts

if there were words. id give you all of them. instead I only have the sinking in my chest as my heart gains weight and sits like a stone on my stomach.

i look at you and see straight through and it stings too much for me to speak. the falling and standing and crawling. the learning to walk again. the loss. the bottom. and our glimmer of hope that there is more for us than. this.

i am human.

and i am learning that you are too. and that's ok. i have to. let you be.   human.

with all its atrocities. all its poison. i have to let you be everything good and bad and in between. i am learning.

to love both. sides. all the sides. to love a house for everything in it.

we have such pretty houses. manicured lawns and posies and art. such pretty houses. but our homes. ..are slightly tussled. ragged. bare. scattered and dirty and falling apart. with leaks and cracks and holes and stains. our closets are filled with skeletons and our rugs lay on top of dust piles big enough to black the sky. enough to understand the sweeping..

but i want to love it all.

and you have helped me see this. have thrown me into the mix where tables turn and there is weakness in each of us.

i want to fix you. but all i can do is just love you. all of you. the best that i can.

and despite my attraction to falling i am praying for the strength to stand, not for me alone, but because i am beginning to better understand.. it is bigger than me. and that...

is worth a heavy heart.

Tuesday, November 13, 2007

the truth is..

i guess you're not as nice as we think you are (the world, my world).   .....and i guess maybe i was right. my feelings. although i never could pin them down before. they would spin. away from me like the world does every time i get close. to figuring it out. to understanding.

it shakes my brain.

to think that maybe i wasn't ever really the fucked up one. i was the only one who saw. who felt. what everyone else wasn't (feeling).

we were all unaffected by everything. you still are.

sticky sweet isn't really sweet at all, and the weather has

nothing to do with the way i screamed at you.

and i guess maybe when you asked me what was so bad, i couldn't ever figure it out. because we were all perfect. to us. in our heads. in the space we created. and i guess what was wrong was that i didn't fit there. that that little world where you were all immune from everything was perhaps, only at my expense.

i think i have you to thank for my news reporter. and the rugs. and the weather. and everything is fine and i have you to thank for that too.

but today it isn't fine. everything is not ok and i am vulnerable and affected by everything. and i have me to thank for that, and these feelings i have here. that i am choosing to feel.

Sunday, November 11, 2007

dont try.

steely eyed rubbish.

and fishoooks.

and bargains. tools. shopping supplies. baskets. groceries. bags. whores. knives.

kites.

we watch movies.

and so are you.

and so am i.

and so are you.

and then it stops and then it starts and wagons. and tissues. and toilet paper.

shortages.

you poop at my apartment.

gas masks. sewer water. disSTILLED water. vomit.

eliot. rides. lots of them.

cereal. spoons. napkins. afternoons and evenings and buddies at places i'm at way too much and they sing for me.

posters and pictures and blurs and dessert.

steak.

steak.

steak.

and mashed potatoes. and i share. for once.

don't expect it ever again. whores.

silly string. popcorn. walls. elbow grease. anger. ants. carpet and vacuum cleaners and i cant spell that word.

bed.

tickles.

snuggles.

laughs. and heart attacks and falling on the floor with your feet in the air and a chair attacking your life with me under the wood and pushing.

screaming.

falls. it falls and i pee a little bit in my pants.

you like it.

mothers and grandfathers and jokes that make you squirm and we're just dumb kids we don't get it anyway. i had to contemplate that one.

it' s for me. and you. and a few laughs on the side and time and dexter and i missed orlando tonight for coffee and family and love and smokes and gifts of birth. stuff.

hookers.

neon signs. fingers. hands. waving. beckoning. no.

happy...brrrrrr...ttthhh....daaaaaa...y.

drunkards.

foxes snakes and holes and fun and lies and standing firm.

falling out of windows.

eating brownies. and dancing in panties and losing things.

spilling. angry. coffee. truck beds. school. hair. faces. grades and lack thereof.

driving.

going.

bieng.

together.

and slugnuts. on the side.

Saturday, August 11, 2007

three letter words could be more powerful than four.
Current mood: amused

YOU, is better than i.
and SHE is even easier. farther away.
SHE is like magic and freedom and masks.
oh! the things WE can be
behind a mask.
YOU is a fly on the wall.
SHE is a story i can tell
with horror and tragedy and unspeakable darkness,
when i have checked out.
YOU allow me to be there.
SHE brings you here. too close. so close
while i am nowhere to be found.
i watch the world be YOU and SHE.

(i watch me)
in wonder.
and wonder when we will speak with i again.
when the trauma will subside.
i weep.
we have been wounded.
oh, when i let YOU or SHE be me it hurts too much.
sets the room spinning.
blacks my sight.
it twists and burns.
"feelings can't kill you"
i remind myself
it doesn't make a difference. i can't tell the difference.
and so i goes back on the shelf, the corner, the vault.
i let me out to breathe every now and then.
they are sharp, painful gasps.
and then SHE comes back and i go away again.
one day.
i will tell a story in first person.
one day i won't be SHE or YOU when i speak
it will be me.

Tuesday, July 24, 2007

on becoming..

we don't know who we are (yet). stripped and humbled and searching, becoming.

broken mirrors and bathroom floors, dark corners and books and locked doors. they do not hold us anymore. (we know this)

oh, there are many things of which i am unsure.

but when i tell you that you are beautiful, my words are not flowers. when i look at you i see a promise. i see a dress of white and know it isn't a lie. know that you are new. and you can.

parallel lines are not supposed to meet but here we are underneath rain clouds on my porch. and something inside of me was asleep, something that your heart has made very much alive.

and with its every beat i am grateful. with your every breath i rest assured.

words, slipped under a door, and my heart's desire has been heard, whispered between the cracks, someone crying with you on the floor.

i sit in awe of the masterpiece, the way the water rippled. i sit there humbled and honored and so undeserving. i sit, with fire.

although we don't know who we are (yet), the becoming is half the fight. oh, the rest is simply doing love, and i know we're going to be alright.

matter

seventeen months and i still show up late. something holds me back. it isn't my heart because it is already there, waiting for me to catch up. she says perhaps it is a matter of mattering.
i shoot her a sideways glance. glare. my eyes find salt and decide to swim.

THIS CYCLE. where there are no expectations. where no one arrives on time if at all. where i am impartial and everything is mostly weightless. MUST BE BROKEN.

how do i make it matter? (and it is me and i'm not sure)

she tells me i do. she has been for (four) years.

what would it take for those words to penetrate? must i be beaten until i feel them, until i believe? surely there's another way..and until then, am i always going to be late?

there is something that feels good there. there is something that makes sense. i'll be tardy because i believe somewhere that i don't matter, and you'll be angry, and then i can feel like a failure.. and we can continue this ugly dance forever.

but i'm tired of tracing myself into cages and boxes and beating her down.

and.

today i am seventeen months old and i am going to do something and show up on time. ....maybe.

Tuesday, July 03, 2007

would you like some waffles with that syrup?....
Current mood: sore

You are sticky sweet and

i

am dismissed.

Swept under the rug

with my foot in my mouth

trying to pull myself together,

i yell at you.

Space is tangled and weighted,

as you talk about the weather.

i am a silly child

and you are *never* angry,

pour your syrup all over me

i'm drowning

in its sweetness.

You are pleasant and untouched

convienently unaware

as i lay wounded at your feet.

It must be my fault,

for you can do no wrong

this burden is mine alone to bear.

my world turns upside down

when i try to look at you,

oh, your fantasy

has caused a split

in me

i'm choking on the truth.

i don't want to live there!

(yes i do.)

But your smile stuffs things away.

Leaves you alone

suprised,

as you **move on** from the decay

(we are always moving on, aren't we? it's what we do best.)

i don't want to discuss the sun

(or the rain or the weatherman, and his faulty predictions)

i want to speak of my *heart...*

i want to make a terrible mess.

...and i don't want you.

to clean it up.

Or pretend it didn't happen.

or paint it pretty

and make it ok..

(**Fuck**! it is **NOT ok**!)

but what would you say..

Friday, June 01, 2007

keys
Current mood: depressed

tonight i had to laugh (all though i felt sad), at the fact, that i had. so. many. keys. to so. many places. i would never be. again.

i found it funny (with my hands fumbling), that my purse, could hold, so many empty homes. as i walk back. to my things packed. again.

found a dog on my bed (and i could not keep mine from my head), waiting, while he is chained, to a stake, in the ground. and i'm praying. it won't be raining.

again.

but i laughed. when i could have cried. because my eyes have dried and i am not ready to be breaking again.

like my fist was not ready to be angry just yet.

like my tank was empty but i was driving because i was not ready to fill it. again.

so when i finally (found the latest key), stepped into new territory, my mind. was. wondering. how long, it would be. before. it happened. again. and then. i had to laugh.

Friday, May 25, 2007

Move.
Current mood: determined

i have been trapped. put on hold. placed carelessly on

layaway. a moment of indecision, confusion, and then i'm left hanging on a wire, suspended. . . . .

how cruel, i say, how unfair! my heart is not mechanical and i don't have a switch to flip. i was not meant to pause, to stop, i am a force that drives that moves and shakes. i am uncomfortable. i am uncertain of many things.

i am uncertain when to fight or flee, when to test or roll over and bare my neck for your teeth to tear to shread or carress. i am uncertain when to stay or take my pieces and go. i am unsure of how this works, how it fits and which parts to discard and which things to hold on to for later. i am unsure of you, your heart and mine and if they match or if i have been coloring outside the lines again.

if i am five and i have dressed myself in all confidence to be laughed back into my bedroom to try again.

or if by going i am burning.

what i am sure of is what my heart is for. the only clarity i find is my drive to move for people. for dirty ditches and reaching hands and shelter in the storms. for setting broken hearts and loving scarred up arms. for building and restoring and tearing down and starting over.

and so that is what i will do. i will move. with or without you. i will walk on and forge this path and let go. open my hand, so sweaty, clenched tight to my chest, and give it back to the one who gave it to me in the first place and trust. (what a heavy word!) in plans for my future, for hope, for a love that will stay.

i will allow you to be removed from me (simple but not easy) and continue forward. and. if, i look over and someone is there, i will run with them.

happily ever after is not always what we thought it would be. is not always guaranteed. is not always. is not... is ....

so this is me hanging up the phone not sure if you have heard, or if you are only listening or if you have again fallen asleep. this is me taking a step forward refusing to turn my head to see if you will choose. to see if you are following me. this is me and my heart determined to move.

(not) disposable.
Current mood: depressed

so. this is what if feels like. to tear apart. this. is what we risk when we throw our hearts out. so this is losing.

i see.

i wish there was truth when i stammered that i didn't care. i wish if i said it enough it would make everything feel better. but it doesn't, and it won't, and the overwhelming powerlessness of sitting through a feeling is keeping me there. in that moment. where it ended.

blink.

half believing if i blink hard enough the things before me will vanish when the shutters fly open. but they don't. they are just sitting there. in the corner. waiting for me.

and then the fury.

if only my fist flying into the door could distract my heart for a moment. if only i could punch its wooden frame hard enough to shake this feeling off. if only..but, who am i kidding? my swollen knuckles weren't meant to be my crucifix.

i never learned how to do this.

so this is what it's like when you finally manage to allow people to matter. they were like sharks' teeth to me. they were disposable.... why couldn't you be? i think i'd like it if, there was something wrong. with me. or you. i think it would make more sense. maybe. if you could yell. or be cruel. intolerable. or if i was a bitch.

i think maybe if you were poisonous i'd let go a little easier.

my sticky fingers make it hard. and somewhere along the lines i somehow fell. and now it's done. it's over. no more stupid fluttery things in my stomach. no more tangled hands. just my tangled heart.

and the question.

is it worth it.

is it.

worth.

this?

yes. (but i'd rather say no.)

Saturday, April 07, 2007

Sirens
Current mood: determined

...Sometimes,
HOPE is a distant shore
that my heart seeks
tossed and battered on an unforgiving
restless sea.
the sirens, the sirens
beckon me in the most beautiful ways
to dash myself upon the rocks,
like the many before me
and many after
have so willingly obeyed.
but
i...
i must reach **her**
that after discovering **her** solid body
i might become
a lighthouse.
oh! to shine in the dark!!
that is the desire that keeps my heart burning
and opens my eyes
against heavy sleep
every sunrise,
though weary and sick i stand
to search endlessly
desperately

for *Hope's* gentle hand.

And i won't say
that there weren't times i lost *her*,
forgot *her* in the struggle to stay afloat,
cursed *her* for being so foreign.

But the sum of my searching has lead me here
to safety. to a new life.

and i would give you my arms
if only they could be god's

i would love you, if only to be a reflection

i would live it transparently
if only to show you the evidence of *hope's* existence,
to give you something tangible to hold onto
when the sirens call.

Monday, April 02, 2007

On Letting Go
Current mood: jubilant

I like to think I can handle it.
I like to hold it in my hands and do with it as I please.
whether it is you, or me, or things.
I like to make plans, and hope, and expect, and get excited.
and.
just when it's in my grasp. it slips. through my fingers.
over.
and over.
and.
over.
how many times does it take?
so today.
I took the thing. that I had held so securely,
crinkled and sweaty in my clenched up palms,
and let it go.
decided to allow someone else to take care of it.
someone else who knew what they were doing.
and pray it would be given back to me.
....

so here's the story.
after chasing cars. for a while.
one disappointment after another.
stress. anger. awe.
i stopped fighting for control.
i turned my will over.
and just when i let it go.
it came back to me.
i have found one. (a carrrrrr)
and it is mine.
yep.
MINE.
I HAVE A CAR.
woooooooooooooooooooooooooooooooooooooooooooooooooooo
ooo....t.
we found it on craigslist.
drove out to see it.
with some cold hard cash.
and.
(my cuteness)
met the guy.
fell in love with the veeeehicle.
competition showed up. hah. no way.
old raggedy man in coveralls.
pssssssssh. you ain't got nooothing on me and my shorts.

so we ran him over with my amazing-ness and stuff and now,
the car is mine.
i am going to be a real person.
who comes and goes as they please.
who drives to your rescue.
who comes over and pulls you out of bed.
who goes to the beach when they want.
who gets milkshakes and cheese fries at three am.
who listens to music and sings with the windows down.
whose airfreshener makes your day better.
who goes to the lake to be alone and think when they want
to.
who is not dependent on you to do anything.
who picks you up when you don't have a ride.
who ran over your dog... oh wait.. no...

hahahha. woooh.
i feel like i have been in a war and my supplies were dwindling,
moral was on a decline, and reinforcements just arrived. i am

refreshed. and joyful. and the growing pains have subsided.
for now.

and i love it.

Friday, March 23, 2007

mirror
Current mood: determined

you can be as ugly as you want
with your claws out
ripping and tearing at me
but i'm not going anywhere.
i will sit here and take it.
if it would show you that i love you.
all of you.

it isn't either, or.
it isn't black or white.
it doesn't fit in the box.
and i don't have pat answers for you.
i won't tell you what you want to hear.
but i will sit here.
and love you.

and i don't have all the answers
so i will just listen.
twist it, turn it around
stab me with it
i won't let you drive me away.

and its funny
because i do the same.

i don't believe if i let the ugliness out
that anyone would love it
hold it
touch it
tell it that it is valuable.
i think i can sit back
sink into the dark comfy corner
and attack anything that attempted to come in.

oh, but look at us.

vile and angry and black
and lovely.

no i wouldn't say the mess is what i love
he didn't say that either
but i love you and there are pieces of you
in all of it.

i see the light in your face
when you are giving.
i see the tenderness
with which you hold those that are dear to you
i see the longing
to be snuggled
because you want to feel the love
that you throw wholeheartedly to anyone that would take it.

i see beneath the black

i see past the glazed over stare you attempt
thinking you can shut that window
if you think dark enough

hurt me.
i'm not going away.

i don't do it the best
i'm learning

make me the rest of the world
everyone who scarred you
and your beautiful heart
i will try to let it roll off my back.

we are not the scars
we are found in the beauty
of their healing.

i don't want your masks
i don't want the cleaned up version
i want you
the parts you would sweep under the rug
the parts that no one has loved
the parts you hate and fight to cover up.

but i do not want to play your games.

oh, and i am listening to myself.

the best that i can.

Monday, March 05, 2007

The bitch
Current mood: drained

that's what we named her.
the girl.
who lives inside of my head
who twists my insides
and clenches down on my throat
she doesn't want me to speak she
storms around
kicking up dirt and dust and shadows
fogging up my brain
and stabbing my temples until i can't see straight.
she closes my eyes and screams
at the thought of my healing
throws temper tantrums
when i feel
she is my autopilot
and my protector
and the wrecker of everything good.
she is a dark storm
that descends swiftly and heavily upon me
and dismisses the good you would offer.
she hugs the thorns and rocks
cherishes them, brings them out for me
to shield me from your love.
when you draw near
she tears through with her claws out
maiming. crippling. destroying.
all she can reach.
and i can't feel my face
it pinches into some horrified form (she says, the listener
who sits on the couch with me)
i am unaware
and she reaches out to touch my cheek and
i can't breathe.
i can't breathe when people touch me.
she says (asks)
it is because i don't know what they are going to do..
i quiver.
my head shakes as the bitch raises, hair standing on end

she says (says)
it is because i have known many bad touches.
oh and then my head is gone away from there my eyes have closed and i wouldn't dare try and come back to that room to that couch. my throat constricts and hatred or fear or pain is lodged in my airway.
"all this fighting, all of this battling, just to accept a compliment!!"
says the bitch. slapping me. beating me down. further and further.
and.
further.
my friend, my listener, sits there with kind soft eyes and beckons me back, and tells me i did good. tells me i fought hard and she is proud. i keep fighting to allow her words to stay there, with me, in my heart and not in my head with the bitch.

the bitch who loves to hate and take and keep me crawling when i want to dance and keep my mouth shut when i want to sing. the bitch who keeps me all alone and hugs me selfishly to herself where she can control and manipulate and enslave.

and to the bitch i say simply..but not easily,
"no.
i want to live."
and wait for god
to sling a rock
at her face.

Tuesday, February 27, 2007

Perception.
Current mood: cranky

i dont want to be seen as a bird.
to be trapped. and kept. and called your own.
i am not something to be caught. i am not some pretty thing.
my eyes are not yours to tame or teach to adore you.

sometimes
i am a storm
to be weathered.

i need you to see me,
the chaos i create..
i need you to see
how self destructive i can be
in my relationships
and gently
love me anyway.

i am not always comparable to roses.
sometimes i am the one who tramples them.

i need you to understand
that when i am silent
it is not always because i haven't any words
but i fear using them
wrongly
i am not always singing.
you can't make me sing for you.

i am volatile.
i am at war with myself and oftentimes
the ones closest to me
are injured in my battles.
should they choose to stay and fight alongside me.

and as much as i want you to stay
i will want you to leave
when you get too close.

and i could tell you a million times but you would never be
prepared
for my running.

i will catch you off guard.
pull you in
and then disappear.

don't let me.

run with me.

i don't want to be seen
as some mystery
for you to solve.
my pieces won't fit in a pretty box for you
and make some reasonable shape.

oh.

i don't belong in a cage.
you cannot trap me.
but you can
love me
and maybe i will allow it
and perhaps
one day i will choose
to love you back.

but not if i am your bird.

Thursday, February 22, 2007

don't ask.
Current mood: nauseated

me how i am. don't try to understand my reactions. actions.
or lack of.
don't get in my way.
i am not rational.
nor do i seem to care right now.
and no. i don't plan on backsliding. I'm not talking about the
easy way out.
thats why it's so hard.
thats why it's all i can do to just. be. today.
just for today.

i don't need more parents.
i don't need you trying to tell me how i am or how i feel.
i'll be the judge of that. (how i feel)
and i don't need you to rob me of the opportunity to make
decisions for myself.

i'm not going to believe anything until it happens.
words are cheap.
actions.
thats what i want.

i dont want promises.
i dont want words.
i want to see it.
SHOW ME.

prove yourself.
i'm waiting for you to prove me right.
and.

you probably will.

but i'm still here.

and so it's back to that.
that place where i just
survive.
where all i can do
is breathe
not pick up
and mechanically move
through the motions.

i have to.
damage control.

i watch too much grays.
and i analyze everything.
too deeply. too long.
and my tongue
lately
has been malfunctioning.
lately
i just hang up
before i say
fuck you
and thank god i just hung up.
lately
i slam the door
and thank god
i didn't punch you in the face.
lately
i sleep too much
and thank god
i can sleep at all
and.
I'm just
moving
forward
hacking my way through vines
that beg to choke me
and hold me back
but that isn't an option.

I'm working on it.

just don't ask.

shit storms.
Current mood: blah

It's easy to get lost in a shit storm.
its easy to forget there were other things before it. better things.
like roses and people and coffee. or your dog.
and sometimes when it's black
it's easy to stay in bed and let the world go on without you
and let the phone ring and pretend you can't hear it.
because i don't want to hear it. (you)
i'd like to think i know how to clean up the mess.
but i don't.
i don't know how. and. supposedly that's ok.

oh. i could wash myself of these things a million times but i'm not sure i would ever feel clean. that they, would ever be clean. to me.
so i move on. replace and refurnish and sing.
hoping the music rising from me will lift the stains.
the dirt.
but what of the ones that won't?
what of the ones that i can't mend?

i don't want to be sick anymore.
i'm ready for the healing.
and.
just when it begins.
the scabs.
they are ripped away. and new wounds are formed.
and
i don't know how. ..

i hide in the covers because i don't know what to put on. for you. because i don't want to put anything on. i just want to be. without you asking me the questions. because they hurt and i don't have answers. i just want to be covered.
..oh and i want someone to hold me when it stabs.
just hold me and don't ask.

and maybe that's the point.
when i manage to pick up the nine million pound phone and call.

and no one answers.
maybe that's the point.
someone is already there with me. who comforts better than
you.
who wishes i'd let them. wishes they could be enough to me
in those moments.
god.
im sorry that i seem to think you're not.
and when i'm crying i call everyone but you.

Tuesday, January 23, 2007

Sleeping
Current mood: determined

i'm sleeping and i can't seem to open my eyes
you've asked me again, and again to pray for your heart
but i have grown weary and i don't know why
wake me up
wake me up
i'm slipping and sliding away from the shore
but you take my hand and you lead me back home
my eyes are heavy from the weight of this world
wake me up
wake me up
we're resting laying locked up in dreams
it's not enough for us just to think
we cannot move and we've lost our sight
wake me up
wake me up
this battle is waging and i've fallen behind
liquid and capsules that love to take me away and
i want to stop bleeding but i don't know how
wake me up
wake me up
i dance in white dresses and speak about love
expose my heart to them humble and broke
we'll weather these storms and together we'll rise
wake up oh sleepers, shrug off the night
wake up oh sleepers, wake up and fight.

Thursday, October 26, 2006

Life is Storms.
Current mood: amused

A storm. Came crashing in. So unexpectedly.. the sun faded out, seemingly sucked into a black hole. It just disappeared. When moments earlier we were laying there, content to soak in its energy, its warmth. It warmed everything inside of us. ...But now it was gone and heavy clouds pregnant with a thousand raindrops have usurped our sky.

Do we forget altogether that there was a sun? No. We know it was there, we know it still is, and we wait. We wait through the thunder and the lightning bold and loud and harsh breaking the canvas above us. We wait through the darkness. Soaking wet and cut off from the world around us. We huddle into blankets and light candles and talk. It is heavy. We hunker down. It can't be like this forever.

And just when we began to lose hope, and give in to the torrential winds, allowing them sweep us away with the dirt and the branches a small beam of light pours through the clouds and it finds us. It finds us sitting there forlorn and laughs at us for nearly giving up. ...and some of us are silly and we think it is over now.. and some of us are wise and we celebrate the rainbow and know that it was necessary. We watch the earth rejoice and grow and new life come to be. We observe those that were dying be revived and strengthened. And we know.

We know that life is storms. Over and over again. Fighting through the downpour. Stretching, growing, and preparing for the next. We are not so naive to think that, that was the last storm, there will be many many more. And we will make it through, if only we fight, and remember what we are fighting for.

Friday, September 29, 2006

hold on to that thread...it gets better.
Current mood: content

sometimes the lies are so much louder. i think that is because they have to be screamed. when, the truth, is quit and still and sits. and waits for you to find it. but when you do it is so powerful. so powerful that in order to survive the lies throw themselves around inside of you with startling intensity ...commence the screaming.

cover your ears. if only you could cover the space between them. ...
well then i guess we wouldn't have a problem, now would we?

don't listen to that voice that rattles inside of your skull. it offers you pretty poison. and empty kiss..es... they will suck you dry and leave you hollow. that blade will cut your heart out. and not in the way you wish it would. it won't leave you numb and tranquil. it will mark the grave with a gaping wound that you can't fill. no. don't be that silly bug. flying to its death, entranced by that lovely light.

BUT INSTEAD.. BELIEVE. with your feet. taking one step at a time. moving steadily forward. crawl. ask to be carried. there are arms waiting to hold you and take you to higher ground. you don't have to drown in this dark sea. FIGHT.

no one ever said it was easy. ...and no one ever asked you to do it alone.

ON A LIGHTER NOTE.
guess who has an apartment now..!!!! acompanied by an amazing roommate, a huge, soft, bed.. furniture, food, AND. a precious puppy who is quickly winning the hearts of the masses. the easily susceptable, the skeptic, the so-called "cat people", the young and the old ....there is no heart he cannot tug. ...his name is johnny, apropriately after johnny cash. and. he is my second chance dog. we are hitting the restart button of life together. haha
someone had thrown him and his other siblings in the woods placed in a garbage bag. he is now cuddled up safely in my room.
sigh.
god is so good.

he who refreshes others will himself be refreshed.

Wednesday, August 16, 2006

I miss you.

sometimes i feel so close to you, and i think i feel you breathing inside of me. and then. sometimes we are so distant and i can't hear you speak to me. i sit outside under your sky and wonder how i let you get so far away and why it is so hard for me to stay... why i always run. and hide. and forget your face. i speak of you. oh, i speak of you all the time. but do i speak to you? and how close can we be if i don't make time. time...and its so easy to get carried off on the ebb and flow but tonight i see so clearly. my thoughts beg to crush me, beat my heart black and blue. i don't want to think. fear. is it going to be fear or faith? am i going to stagnate or make a change and leeeeap. off of this cliff and walk on water. no. it isn't safe. but it is where i want to be.

arrrrrrgh.

Monday, August 14, 2006

funny-ness. and good friends.

Me: "Renee, you get all the looks."
You: "It's the boots and short shorts. Even a dog would look. A dog would walk by and look, a pig too. It's not me."

you're too sexy for me. - Steph

i just looked through some of my comments and found this. hahhahha. i love my friends. they make me laugh so hard. i am apartment hunting again tomorrow. so wish me luck.

Sunday, August 13, 2006

life. is. strange.
Current mood: sad

he was broke and he broke my little heart and our eyes, our eyes, they meet and mine, were swimming and yours were hollow and they scratched my soul. oh, i should have been a doctor so i could fix you but i can't and my black face will not help but it is yours my friend because i know so intimately where you've been. OH GOD i know and i hope that those holes will get filled before your heart falls out. like i hoped that my tooth would get fixed before it came out...and it did, it did, oh please don't fall apart. little heart, little heart, why are you breaking? because i prayed i begged i said, oh god let what breaks your heart break mine too and here it goes spilling down my cheeks and making streams and i'll just leave them there. let them sit. and soak. and show. let it show let it all air out there's no need for closets anymore.

and the music is so beautiful it makes me want to die. and the moon is bright and shining and wonderful and the stars are streaking across the sky and it just feel wrong for the world to be so lovely when it has so many broken people falling apart inside.

i want to scoop them up, and hold them in the palms of my hand and lift them into the air, back into your arms. i'd turn my face and scream the pain away and find some peace in knowing they are your children anyway.

and as i shake i see the glaring green print on the sign infront of me. COKE. it says. it speaks of beer. ..and i have to laugh. nice try, nice try. ill have none of that oh no, i won't be fucking up this time. I'll give you credit though, it was a valiant effort. so i light my cigarette and swallow what seems like half the bottle of my coffee and catch a glimpse of my silly face and all its stains and i like it. it is honest.

oh, i just want to be honest. and it hurts and it tears and then you must sing. you must let it come flowing out from your mouth and sweetly lifting through the air. like a detox you project all of the dirt onto those notes and let them go.

but he was looking. his eyes were so greedy and they touched me in such a way i wanted to go home and scrub them off of me. why. why do you devour me so shamelessly, and then i realize that he is needy. just like me. and you. and everyone. and we are far from perfect. and it's scary. and i wonder does he cry? does he go home all alone and feel empty inside. and he is once again every one of them and i think of them all. and cry for their hearts. and plead for the hatred to leave, and beg for forgiveness and grace. and love. and lord, i know, i know it will come.

so lift your face little ones, up away from the darkness below you and breathe. breathe again and remember there is more. remember life is strange. and remember what we are living for. ....remember what we are living for.

Wednesday, August 02, 2006

crash and burn.
Current mood: crushed

it's not just him. it's every one of them. it is every ugly memory turning in my stomache and scratching up my throat. it is a down pour of pain, pitter patter down my porclain face streaking tearing, diving down my chin again and again. it is puncture wounds inside my soul and dark caverns with murky pools stirring and rising to drench me from head to toe in a tidal wave of foolish thoughts. and "what if" and "maybe" and i think i could it would be so much easier to cave to crawl and fuck it all and give in, give up, fuck up fuck up and my heart is screaming   NO. but my arms are begging, "oh please, oh pretty please, release release, release it unto me" and i feel sick and. it. is vomit in my mouth and i hate this. and my silly addict self and why couldn't i just make it go away, why couldn't i just slide a bit today...oh no, oh no. and i know it would never go away. god. OH GOD come and meet me in this dark place and hold me. hold me like i want to be held and take this weight away. take the blade away and take this pain and help me learn how to face. it. and not to run away but to refrain from these irrational escapes. oh father guide me i am blind and i am hurting and my stupid head is pleading to turn back. ..and the only thing i know in this pit is that you won't leave my side. ...you wont leave my side. my side. you are on my side and i, i wont let go and i wont let go and carry me please i am too weak but you are so much bigger than me and this and him and them and we can walk through it...only when i becomes we and me becomes him, only then. and only then. ....i will not give in.

Saturday, July 15, 2006

I haven't written anything in a while..some ranting and raving. madness really.

Current mood: contemplative

I am not a pretty picture.

I am not a project or something for you to fix. I am a beautiful mistake, I am a mess, I am tragedy I am fairytales. I am a story, as are you, and with every line across my wrist I was screaming and with every tear that I shed I am praying for me and you and "them" and us. We are not alone we are in this together and I am on my face tonight. And darkness screams behind the door, it is begging, fighting to get in.

THIS IS WAR.

And I will not let it in, I will not succumb to your sweetness. I will not be betrayed by the kiss of a blade by the liquid that gives to take and I, I will not swallow those lies that sit on my plate. Break. Shatter. Collide and fall. Pretty poison. I used to think I should come with a warning label, I thought I destroyed everything that I touched and now, now I see, now I know it was not me it was the Hole it was the monster that came in and wrecked everything I know...and love...and love and hope would not let me go. And love and hope grew arms to reach me when I was running and wrap me snug in a hug that my heart had longed for oh so long. And love and hope in stars and hearts on my back on my arms and in my heart as mine, for me to give to you and that is what the pain was for. And that was worth it all, and more.

Friday, August 25, 2006

HAPPY BIRTHDAY DARLING.
Current mood: ecstatic

NO. IT ISN'T MY BIRTHDAY. as in. i wasn't literally, physically born on the 24th of this month. however, this date, marks six months of a new life for me. this date marks six months that i have not chased my pain away with a razor blade. six months that i have not drowned out the memories in my head with a bottle. six months that i have not sought to escape myself in some drugged out alternate universe...

i am not perfect. i am not a hollywood story where all the ends are tied up neatly and explained. but i am learning, and growing and allowing myself to be loved and to love like never before. i am learning to live deliberately. to be a light in dark places. to have what breaks god's heart break mine too.

this isn't easy. the attacks are so sly, so cunning and baffling, and powerful. but my god is bigger than that. it's funny. somehow i forget and think i am alone....but tonight, i came home to read comment after comment of people praying, encouraging, telling me that they are there with me. ...an answer to a prayer that i have only recently begun praying... that people would know what i am about...and here is my answer. ...

i hung on. i clung to life and hope in the darkest of times when there didn't seem to be any reason, and it was all so distant...i refused to let go because i knew that god would use my pain to bring healing to others. i only have one life to live, and i want to use it. to be a cracked vessel, to be available and willing to do whatever i am called. i want to jump in the muddy trenches with people who want out and help show them the way. i want to love with the same love that i have been shown. ..to be a shining star in the universe.

i didn't do this of my own accord, i am not that strong. god has carried me so many times when all i could do was lay there in my bed begging him to help me get through the moment, the urge to destroy everything, he drew near to me. through a friend, a pet, a song....a hug deep inside of my heart.

oooh. i got that keytag and i never wanted to let it out of my palm. it was hard work getting to this point. ....but it happened, and it can happen for anyone who wants it.

this isn't my story. this is God's story of redemption, being used to redeem others.....how beautiful is that.